CLASSIC
IRISH
WHISKEY

In the same series:

CLASSIC
IRISH
WHISKEY

JIM MURRAY

Dedication

To my mother
Mary Hannah Elizabeth Murray
my lifelong purveyor of tender encouragement
who entered this world in 1921
as a Crimins.
Also, to all long lost Irish members
of that family, whoever, wherever
they may be.

First published in Great Britain in 1997 by PRION BOOKS LIMITED
32-34 Gordon House Road London NW5 1LP

Reprinted 1998

A previous edition of this book was published in 1994 as *Jim Murray's Irish
Whiskey Almanac* by Neil Wilson Publishers

© PRION BOOKS LIMITED 1997
Text copyright © Jim Murray 1994, 1997
Editorial coordination by Lynn Bryan
Designed by Jill Plank

A CIP catalogue record for this book is available from the British Library.
ISBN 1 85375 241 X

Printed and bound in China by
Sino Publishing Ltd.

CONTENTS

PREFACE
TO FIRST EDITION

For a people so friendly and who, in any of the thousands of bars that can be found in every village and town throughout the land, will engage you in lively debate on any topic under the sun and expound their views with a courteous freedom, the Irish are also very fond of keeping their secrets.

Until the publication of this book, perhaps their biggest secret of all was Irish whiskey. While the rest of the world has been allowed to sample only Jameson and Bushmills as works of the Irish distiller's art, the Irish have been able to rejoice daily in the latter-day *uisce beatha*, the water of life, which although not aiming to challenge the best established whiskeys in the world, is unquestionably their peer.

Who in Britain, the USA, France, Japan, Germany, Australia, New Zealand or any other whiskey-drinking nation has ever been fortunate enough to discover the truly astonishing delights of a Power's or a Redbreast: two whiskeys with such succulent pot still character that you nose and drink a part of Ireland's very soul every time you put them to your lips? Regrettably, few people have had the chance.

Opposite

Native two row Irish barley ready for harvest. It is the use of unmalted barley that gives Irish its distinctly lighter character compared to Scotch.

Opposite
The pure,
crystal waters
of Ireland
help make
Irish whiskey
what it is.

This, quite remarkably, is the first book ever to take a drinker on a detailed tour around all Ireland's whiskeys, no matter how common or obscure. Other books have been written on Irish whiskey but they covered only its turbulent history, never its produce. I have ensured that *Classic Irish Whiskey* has gone beyond that historical perspective. My single aim in this book is to act as a personal guide to anyone who wishes to know something, not only about its history, but also (and perhaps more importantly to those who will be spending good money on a bottle!), the character of the whiskey and why it tastes the way it does. After all, no whiskey in the world is made in such a complicated manner as the Irish variety and for the first time some of the secrets of why Irish whiskey has such a distinctive flavour will be revealed.

The reader may not agree with all my tasting notes. But I am sure he or she will understand my standpoint and use these notes either to try out or stay away from certain brands. Whiskey is an expensive commodity and thus my impartiality should help you in selecting what suits you best.

I have written more in newspapers and magazines than any other writer on Irish whiskey and not always through shamrock-tinted spectacles. Irish Distillers know I will never be content until they make more of their better brands available throughout the world. I hope this book awakens people's interest so that it is not only me pleading to give pot still a chance. But I cannot be too harsh; Irish Distillers is a commercial enterprise and must

put its money where it will most bear fruit. And they do produce some wonderful whiskeys which I have tried not to make too wonderful for words! I am lucky. My work as a whiskey writer takes me to distilleries all over the world and there is something special about Ireland. It may be my Irish blood from a couple of generations back; it may be the softly contoured land of pastel greens; it may be the warmth of the people; it may be the enchantment felt by the discovery of yet another facet of a whiskey you thought you already intimately knew. It is probably all those things. Through the pages of this book I want to take you on a special journey and share my very good fortune with you.

Jim Murray, 1994

PREFACE
TO SECOND EDITION

Two years is a long time for whiskey. When my first Irish Whiskey book was published in November 1994 it contained the history and tasting notes of every Irish whiskey brand in existence, a number just short of 50. When this revised edition was completed in November 1996 that number had doubled!

After years in the doldrums Irish again has the wind in its sails and has become the fastest growing of the world's whiskeys with Jameson nudging through the magic one million case a year barrier for the first time. Throughout Britain and North America Irish bars have sprung up selling Irish ales and stouts and, naturally, Irish whiskey. No self-respecting town is without an Irish pub and a new generation has now discovered the relaxing delights of the "craic" and more Irish whiskey is being tried and ultimately enjoyed. That is not surprising: there is no doubt that Irish whiskey is better now than it was in 1994.

Some people have very kindly suggested my book had a little to do with this, insofar as certain brutal comments I made about one or two brands made the distillers take stock of what they were doing. If that is the case, I am flattered. But it is the emergence of the Cooley Distillery near Dundalk over those two years which I believe has made Irish Distillers focus their minds on just what potential they have. Off the record, one or two senior people at Irish Distillers are glad of Cooley's continued independence as for the first time in 30 years we are beginning to see just how truly great Irish whiskey can be with companies like Irish Distillers bringing out new whiskeys, including – for me – a top five world-ranking gem like Jameson Gold.

A by-product of this has been my inability to be quite so vitriolic in my condemnation of bad Irish whiskeys, simply because they are now so hard to find. Even the standard though still disappointing Bushmills White Label seems to be getting better each time I sample it and blender Barry Walsh has promised me that by the time of the third edition I won't have anything negative to say about it all. Admittedly, a number of the Cooley blends are something of a muchness heading towards the bland, but you cannot be particularly scathing as the whiskeys used are sound and it is rare to find any off-notes whatsoever. But, like Irish Distillers, they produce some absolute crackers and hopefully this book will introduce you to them.

So, for anyone either just starting out on their discovery of Irish whiskey, or indeed, on their second lap already, I hope this book remains a constant companion and guide.

Jim Murray, February 1997

CHAPTER ONE

WHISKEY'S ORIGINS

INEVITABLY, NO MATTER IN HOW DETAILED OR BRIEF A MANNER YOU TELL THE STORY OF IRISH WHISKEY THE READER WILL BE SEARCHING FOR AN ANSWER TO THE OBVIOUS QUESTION: WHEN DID IT ALL BEGIN?

Unless an ancient document, previously undiscovered, comes to light regarding the origins of distilling in Ireland, a single fact will always remain: nobody really knows. Over the years there have been many claimed instances of Irish whiskey being mentioned in ancient texts. But, to date, all my researches have drawn a blank. Stories which have been accepted as the truth and recounted in many books, booklets and pamphlets all founder on the hard rocks of fact and few of them stand up to close scrutiny.

A problem with the telling of tales down through the centuries is that they tend to be romanticized, or bent and moulded into a shape which will be most appreciated by the targeted listener or reader. Frequently these stories serve merely as commercial propaganda. It has ever been thus with Irish whiskey. It has been claimed, for instance, even by the great whiskey guru of the late

WHISKEY AND HEALTH.

As is well known to the Medical Faculty, the importance of age and purity in Whiskey cannot be over-estimated.

Of **GEO. ROE'S** Celebrated **"GR"** WHISKEY "The British Medical Journal" writes: —

"It has a soft and mellow taste, evidently produced by ageing, and altogether the **'GR'** Whiskey is of excellent quality."

And this statement has been endorsed by members of the Medical Profession.

This Pure POT-STILL WHISKEY may be had in Bottle, bearing the Distiller's guarantee of PURITY and AGE, SEVEN YEARS OLD, from all Wine and Spirit Merchants and Hotel Proprietors in the United Kingdom.

Price 3s. 6d. per Bottle. In Cases of 2 Gallons (Carriage Paid), 42s.

THE DUBLIN DISTILLERS' CO., LIMITED, THOMAS STREET DISTILLERY.
(GEO. ROE & CO., DUBLIN.)
Readers of this Magazine have already been offered an opportunity of testing this Fine Old Whiskey Free.

Left
Here's to your health – this turn-of-the-century advertisement for George Roe uses the British Medical Journal to endorse the purity of its product.

19th and early 20th century, J A Nettleton, that it was first mentioned by soldiers of Henry II when they invaded Ireland in 1174. But Nettleton only appeared to be aping the equally great Samuel Morewood, whose gloriously titled *A Philosophical and Statistical History of the Inventions and Customs of Ancient and Modern Nations in the Manufacture of Inebriating Liqueurs* of 1838, is still, in my opinion, the best work of its kind ever written. Although Morewood painted a vivid picture of drinking the world over, he was a Dubliner who was naturally given to venting national pride.

So far, I have been unable to discover the source of Henry II's alleged connection with whiskey. The most likely candidate to have had such knowledge would have been Giraldus De Barri, now known as Gerald of Wales; then simply as Cambrensis, a monk of breathtaking self-importance who was close to the king and whose own relations took part in the invasion. Cambrensis's dislike of the Irish bordered on the manic and in his first book on them and the country, *The History and Topography of Ireland* (*Topographia Hibernica*), he was at pains to describe them as "treacherous, cruel, dishonest" – and those were the kinder insults. If he could find any fault with them he would. Oddly, though, at no stage did he mention any habit of drinking *uisce beatha*, the Celtic word meaning "water of life" and which eventually came to be known as whiskey. He talks about an abundance of wine being available, all of it imported and much milk and honey, but he does not mention ale or even distilled ale, which would have been the forerunner to whiskey.

Soon after his *Topographia Hibernica* was published, by popular demand Cambrensis wrote an account in 1188 of Henry II's conquest of Ireland, the *Expugnatio Hibernica*. And again, though going into great detail and taking delight in repeating many of the insults he had already heaped on the Irish people, the habit of making or drinking whiskey was not amongst them. In fairness to this revered monk (revered outside Ireland, that is), he did make observations on their way of life beyond the bestial and it does seem strange that had whiskey-making been in evidence, he chose not to mention it.

My research eventually led me to the unlikely setting of Merton College, the oldest seat of learning in Oxford. There they have an original copy of the 14th-century work entitled *Rosa Anglica*, by John of Gaddesden, the foremost physician of his day who was mentioned in the prologue of Chaucer's *Canterbury Tales*, and for the next three centuries the standard work which all physicians consulted. Apparently, there is in existence a 15th-century Irish translation in which the word "whiskey" appears and is described as being used as a tool to aid the healing of paralysis

Left
Gerald of Wales's (c. 1146-1223) failure to mention uisce beatha *in his scathing yet detailed accounts of Ireland offers further evidence to dispel the commonly held view that whiskey originated in Ireland.*

of the tongue: "Rub the tongue and wash frequently with whiskey...Let the whiskey be rubbed often on the back of the head, the tongue and the paralysed limb..."

However, on searching through the original edition at Merton, where Gaddesden himself studied, I could find no reference at all to whiskey. Instead, in the hand-written Latin, it appears as *aqua vitae* which also means "water of life". Furthermore, Gaddesden actually revealed how to prepare aqua vitae. It was made from wine, not grain, and although herbs were added to form a compounded liquor, cereal grains such as barley and oats, were not.

Likewise, beware that some books suggest that when Sir Thomas Savage, who overlorded the lands which now include Bushmills Distillery, fortified his troops prior to battle with the English by topping them up with "Uisce Beatha". It was in fact aqua vitae, according to the noted Elizabethan Thomas Campion. In any case, noblemen like Savage would have drunk wine as a matter of habit, regarding aqua vitae as too coarse and beneath their station.

Tall tales with foundations as soft and murky as an Irish peat bog are all that exist of the earliest popular stories regarding Irish whiskey. For years I was of the opinion that the art of distillation had been brought to Scotland from Ireland by the early Christian holy men of those dark ages between the retreat of the Romans and the invasion of England by the Normans. As my investigations continued, so those beliefs began to vanish. I was surprised to discover that not only was there no mention whatsoever of distillation in the ancient Irish Brehon laws, but there was not even a word for such common distilling artefacts as "still" or "still worm" in the Irish language.

But this is, after all, a subject of some confusion and contradiction. I have stated already that Cambrensis made no mention of distilling or brewing. How does that tally, then, with the fact that the brewing of ale in Ireland is clearly recorded by Jonus in his *Life of St Columbanus* written between 589 and 640AD? "When the hour of refreshment approached, the minister endeavoured to serve about the ale which is bruised from the juice of wheat and barley..." So if Cambrensis is mistaken here, or simply did not bother to record the practice, could the same be said for distilling?

While Cambrensis had some strange and unpleasant stories to tell about the people of Erin, he does not pick up on a story told in the *Annals of Ulster* of 1013 which mentions people drinking themselves to death, although the deadly liquor is not named. Two annals written long after the time of Cambrensis, the *Annals of the Four Masters* and the *Annals of Clonmacnoise* independently tell the same story about Richard Magranell. In the latter: "1405AD, Richard Magranell, chieftain of Moyntyreolas, died at Christmas by taking a surfeit of aqua vitae...it was not aqua vitae to him but aqua mortis." This is the first mention of aqua vitae in any of Ireland's ancient documents. But, again, there is no evidence of the distilling of grain spirit unlike Scotland, where in the year 1494, the first mention of whiskey is made. In the Scottish Exchequer Rolls is found the following entry: "To Friar John Cor, by order of the King, to make aquavitae, viii bolls of malt..." Here both aqua vitae and malt are mentioned together: an irrefutable case. For real proof, the Irish have to wait longer. An Act of Parliament passed in Drogheda in 1556 and referred to in 1620 states "...in Ireland, for the prices of wines extends not to aqua vitae, but there is a statute made in the fourth yeare of Phillip and Mary, here in Ireland...that recites the consumption of graine in making of aqua vitae, and that it is not profitable daily drunk...under paine of Imprisonment at the Deputie's pleasure..."

What is clear is that by the early Tudor period there was concern about the effects which grain aqua vitae (whiskey) was having on the Irish population. This was underlined through by-laws introduced in Galway in 1585: "That a more straighter order be taken to barr the making of aqua vitae of corn than hereunto hath beene used, for that the same is a consumation of all the provition of corne in the Commonwealth. That the aqua vite that is sould in town ought rather to be called aqua mortis to poyson the people than comfort them in any good sorte." But could these measures not have been made in the self-interest of wealthy merchants? Galway was a major port which did such an amount of business with Spain that a Spanish quarter grew up within the town. And one of the principle imports from Spain was wine. It seems certain, therefore, that the making and drinking of whiskey was widespread throughout Ireland by the 16th century. The art of distillation was known in Ireland by the 14th century, and possibly before by monks for the purpose of healing. The making of ale was common practice by 600AD, so despite the fact that neither Bede nor Cambrensis felt fit to mention this remarkable alchemy, it might be assumed that somewhere between the year 600AD and the 1300s the two crafts of brewing and distilling were carried out together. Incidentally, the undated *Red Book of Ossory*, thought to be 14th-century, also mentions the art of distilling wine. If the monks did make aqua vitae from grain, they kept quiet about it. So did merchants, as according to Morewood, in 1300 wheat, oats, malt and ale were exported to Scotland to replenish Edward I's army. Aqua vitae, whether derived from grain or wine, was not listed.

It remains an enigma, one over which I shall continue to puzzle and to which one day I hope to find an answer.

NB: By convention, the "ky" spelling of whisk(e)y refers to Scotch, Canadian and Japanese whisky/whiskies. Everything else, including Irish, is "key/keys". However, brand-owners occasionally opt for the form that is not typical in their local industry. Old Midleton, for instance uses "ky".

CHAPTER TWO

DISTILLING HISTORY

THE PERIOD BETWEEN THE LATE 16TH CENTURY AND THE EARLY 19TH CENTURY WAS ONE OF EXTREME CONFUSION WITH REGARD TO THE MAKING AND DISTILLING OF IRISH WHISKEY.

Then, English-based governments saw the increase in the popularity and availability of this spirit as one of the main reasons for the continuing civil unrest. At the same time it was realized by those governments that there were benefits to be had from this widespread craft.

It is perhaps surprising that as the making of whiskey flourished in Ireland during the reign of Elizabeth I, 1558-1603, (who was apparently quite fond of it), the queen, whose household was in a permanent state of financial difficulty, did not recognise a new opportunity to raise revenue from taxing distilling.

Instead, it was not until Christmas Day 1661 that the Government gave the people a present they hardly wanted – a tax of four pence on every gallon of whiskey distilled. Poteen-making began on the Boxing Day! With immediate effect, a new Government department was set up in Dublin:

Opposite

Cowan's – one of the many now extinct Irish brands. With so many distilleries, merchants and bottlers, constant mergers and take-overs the history of whiskey in Ireland is often confusing.

the Excise. For the first 100 years the department had very limited success. Distillers would declare only what they could get away with, while many declared nothing at all and took to the hills to make their spirit. Corruption was rife, with MPs and powerful landowners able to produce what they wanted tax-free, or undertake to collect the duty from others and divert it into their own pockets. In 1761 the Excise Department, or Revenue Board as it was known, was revamped. It had more powers than of old and more teeth to bare. Until 1823 the scene in Ireland was in a constant state of flux with the rates of taxation being changed, it seemed, every other month. With distillers bogged down in regulations, those who became either too entangled in them, or avoided them altogether, faced fines and imprisonment if the Excisemen, the "gaugers", found them out.

In that year an Act of Parliament was passed to make distilling a much simpler and more equitable affair for those with bigger stills, and an outright illegal one for those with stills which held less than 40 gallons. Anything smaller was considered small enough to conceal.

The making of illicit and legal whiskey had never been so far apart. By the end of the 18th century there were some 2,000 stills in operation in Ireland where whiskey had now become their national spirit in a very big way.

Morewood, on opening his section on drinking in his homeland underlined this point with the

comment: "In Ireland...distilling is carried out to a greater extent than any other portion of the world of equal magnitude and...forms a branch of great commercial importance and enterprise..."

Indeed it did. Some who decided to distil legally tried to raise the capital to set themselves up as large concerns. The most successful were the four big Dublin distillers: John Power, John Jameson, George Roe and William Jameson. Theirs was considered the finest whiskey in all Ireland. Along with other Irish distillers' exports, their products were sold throughout the British Empire and

beyond and their success was boosted quite unexpectedly when the phylloxera vastatrix louse decimated the vines in the Cognac region of France in 1872 making French wines and particularly brandy almost impossible to obtain.

Irish whiskey then outsold its Scottish counterpart on account of the unmalted barley used exclusively in Irish whiskey thus making it a lighter spirit. Both Irish and Scotch became popular drinks with the moneyed classes as stocks of brandy dried up and the pre-prandial became a Scotch or Irish and soda. But as Irish whiskey appeared to be on the verge of taking the world

market by storm, four totally unconnected events took a stranglehold on its progress.

The first occurrence was in the unlikely form of a Capuchin Friar, Father Mathew, who, during the 1840s and 50s swept through the country turning people against what he perceived as the evils of the demon drink. Temperance societies were set up in their hundreds throughout Ireland and sinners, seeing the error of their ways, and no doubt with much encouragement from their long-suffering wives, were persuaded to turn their backs on whiskey, beer and stout for ever. Such was the fever pitch at his rallies that in two visits to Dublin he claimed to have signed up 75,000 converts to his Total Abstinence Movement. When he began the crusade in 1838 there were some 21,000 drinking outlets in Ireland and more money was being spent on drink than was good for the Irish economy and its people's health. However, within six years of his work commencing, that number was down by more than a third to just over 13,000. The small, provincial distiller began to look financial ruin in the face.

The second came with the development of blended whiskey. Ironically it was a French-born Irishman and exciseman Aeneas Coffey and to a lesser extent a Scot, Robert Stein, who worked in a Dublin distillery, who accidentally set the ball rolling. Coffey had tried to sell to the Irish distillers his design for a far more efficient continuous still which made cheaper grain spirit, but contained far less flavour. They rejected his proposals out of hand since they desired to keep Irish whiskey light but full flavoured and produced by the traditional pot still method.

Meanwhile in Scotland, a spirit merchant by the name of Andrew Usher, an agent for The Glenlivet

Opposite
Barley being delivered to Jameson's Bow Street Distillery in 1919.

26

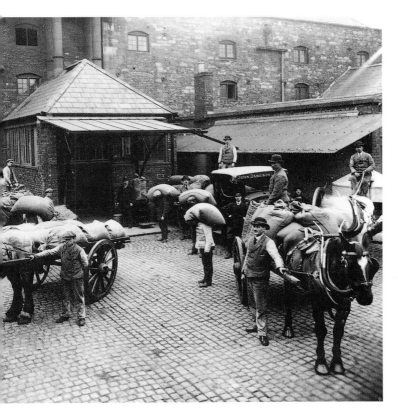

Distillery, had no such reservations. Usher experimented with a mixture of Scottish malt whisky and grain whisky from a Coffey still to produce a number of blends, one of which, Green Stripe, is still produced today.

His commitment to the new process, around 1853, was the green flag for other blenders like

Dewar and Buchanan to begin to sell their whiskies around the world. The age of the "whisky baron" had begun.

But in Ireland there was no such progress. They looked upon blended whisky with outright disdain, but suddenly became caught up with its effects when their export sales began losing out to

Scotch, as the Scottish blends were known, and because the very whiskey which they went to such pains to protect was being sold by middle men as blends of traditional pot still and grain whiskey.

The situation became so bad that in 1879 the four Dublin distillers joined forces to publish a book called *Truths About Whisky* (sic). Very often people ordering Irish whiskey had been shocked to discover that it was relatively tasteless. In fact the blenders, without the distillers consent, had been using perhaps only 20 per cent pot still whiskey in the make-up. The book called for the banning of this practice. Part of their defence was the fact that the Scottish Bo'ness Distillery Company sued Londonderry publican John Magee for refusing to pay for a cask of whiskey which he claimed was adulterated.

"The order of the cask from the Company's Belfast agent, and its delivery in the usual way, having been proved, the defendant said that he had opened the cask the day he had got it, and gave about a glass and a half of the spirit to a boy named Bradley. After drinking it Bradley leaped clean up off the ground, then threw himself down

Opposite
Matured casks of Jameson's ready to go off for bottling.

on his mouth and nose, and endeavoured to knock his brains out. When lying on the ground he wanted to eat the flesh of his arms..." The inference by the authors was that a spirit made in Ireland, perhaps from potatoes, had been added to the whisky.

Although the magistrate found in favour of the publican, a Government commission designed to sort out the "What is Whisky?" question decided that grain spirit could also be called whisky provided it was matured for long enough. From then on the Irish distillers had an uphill battle against the Scotch producers and only Cork Distilleries seemed keen on marketing a blend, although with little of the zeal that had gone into the by now world-famous Scotch brands.

Even so, Irish whiskey still had a healthy market in many parts of the Empire and the United States. But those, too, were soon to be lost. The US market was placed beyond them by the enforcement of Prohibition in 1920 which continued until 1933. Only comparatively small amounts managed to breach the blockade. Worse still, the Irish War of Independence in 1916 culminated first in the partitioning of the country and then in civil war between 1919 and 1921. When a trade war began between the new Free State and Britain, the Irish whiskey industry was going to be a sure-fire casualty. The British and Empire markets including Canada, South Africa, Australia, New Zealand and India were from that date beyond the Irish distillers' reach.

Many distilleries died out. For some like Monasterevan and Wexford, death was quick. For others, like Locke's, Comber and Tullamore it was slow, stretching into the mid-1950s. By the time the trade embargoes had ended and Prohibition had been repealed only a few distilleries like John Jameson and Power's had sufficient stocks to try to rekindle the market. But their commercial strength had been greatly weakened and an entire generation had passed by without tasting Irish whiskey. There was plenty of Scotch, though, taking its place.

In 1966, however, a momentous decision was reached. The few remaining distilleries in the Republic, Jameson, Power's and Cork Distilleries decided to combine forces to create the Irish Distillers Company. Their aim was to pool their resources and fight for a decent share of the world whiskey market.

It was not the first time distilleries had joined forces in this way. Cork Distilleries had begun as a merger of a number of distilleries, and when Irish Distillers acquired Ulster's last distillery, Bushmills in the early 1970s, every Irish whiskey brand was being marketed under one corporate banner. But Irish whiskey as a whole was stationary. The Irish Distillers Group had a very unimpressive track record in that most vital of sales areas, export. It was regarded in Ireland as a company performing well below expectations and was often criticized. As the company grew weaker a takeover bid became inevitable.

Opposite
The Old
Bushmills
Distillery in
Co. Antrim,
now part of
Irish Distillers
and home to
some of the
highest-profile
Irish brands in
the world.

Between 1987 and 1989 Irish Distillers found themselves in the centre of the most dramatic tug-of-war in the Republic's industrial history. On the one hand was a company known as GC&C Brands which was jointly owned by two established Irish companies, Gilbey's of Ireland and Cantrell & Cochrane (Guinness had teamed up with them to strengthen the bid).

These companies were already the subsidiaries of two giant British concerns: Grand Metropolitan and Allied Lyons, but the successful buyer after a number of bruising business encounters was Pernod-Ricard. On their victory, the last four members of the old distilling families of Dublin and Cork resigned.

Had GC&C won, the brands would have been broken up into two camps: Gilbey's on the one hand and Cantrell & Cochrane backed by Guinness on the other. That would have meant massive marketing of a number of whiskey brands throughout the world. Instead, Pernod-Ricard decided upon a policy of putting all their marketing clout behind Jameson and Bushmills on the world stage, leaving the others almost exclusively for home consumption. The monopoly was set to continue.

However, that is not the case now with the emergence of the Cooley Distillery near Dundalk. Irish Distillers tried to take over and close down the Co. Louth distillery and while doing so they off-loaded their Tullamore Dew brand to Cantrell & Cochrane. Again, Irish distillers have to fight it out in the market amongst themselves. But the market has changed, as people's perceptions and expectations have moved a little higher.

Irish whiskey, whether it be from Midleton, Cooley or Bushmills, is at last being seen again for what it was clearly recognized as over a century ago: a very high-class product of great finesse. Now all of these distillers must work hard to ensure that the future will be a lot kinder to Irish whiskey than its past.

CHAPTER THREE

MAKING WHISKEY

T HERE IS A POPULAR MISCONCEPTION REGARDING IRELAND AND ITS MOST GLORIOUS PRODUCT. AND MAYBE THE FACT THAT IT IS A WHISKEY-MAKING COUNTRY HAS HELPED CONFUSE MATTERS.

Many people believe Irish whiskey is made in similar conditions to those in Scotland. That may be true to an extent up at Bushmills in Co. Antrim, just a couple of miles from a pounding sea where drizzle seems to hang in the air and to a lesser degree at Cooley, a distillery that nestles in the foothills of the mountains of Mourne. But it is certainly not true at the greatest of Ireland's distilleries, Midleton in Co. Cork.

Just a few miles along the road to the east of the city, Midleton sits on the same latitude as Hitchin near London, rather than the Scottish Highlands. The sea laps nearby but there are no mountains, just gentle hills and the occasional palm tree thriving in the serenity of the Gulf Stream breeze. Snow falls but a few days in winter, rarely lying for long on the ground and the warehouses in which the whiskey is stored are often clammy and humid rather than dank and freezing.

Opposite
State-of-the-art dinosaurs – the vast swan-necked pot stills in the high-tech stillhouse at the Midleton distillery are reminiscent of grazing brontosauruses.

Opposite William Jameson's Marrowbone Lane Distillery in Dublin c. 1880. The Jameson's brands are now produced at Irish Distillers' Midleton complex in Co. Cork.

You would expect, then, the fruits of Midleton's giant stills to be markedly different to anything produced elsewhere, and they are. But, oddly, although the temperate weather does have some effect on maturation and the outcome of the whiskey, it is the distilling practice carried out within the complex which has the biggest say in its character. In Scotland it could be argued that the wood in whisky maturation has the greatest influence overall: not so at Midleton.

I can think of no other distillery in the world which is as complex as the plant in Co. Cork. When the new distillery was designed and built it had to produce a range of whiskeys which, when blended, would form similar characters to the original whiskeys produced at Jameson's in Bow Street, Power's of John's Lane, the original Midleton and, to some extent, Tullamore.

By the time the new distillery opened in March 1975 things had already been made a lot easier. For a start the type of whiskey was now lighter in style with much of the heavy oiliness removed. This process had been adopted in the late 1960s by all the distilleries as they battled to improve quality control and also their standing amongst

whiskey drinkers throughout the world who preferred the perceptibly cleaner Scotch. Also, the content of the pot still was now simply the mash from malted and unmalted barley. That had not always been the case.

During the late 19th and early 20th centuries five types of grain were commonly used: malt as 30-50 per cent by weight, barley as 30-40 per cent, oats as 20-30 per cent, wheat as 5-10 per cent and rye as 3-6 per cent. Because of this low amount of malted barley, the mashing process, where the ground grain is mixed with hot water, used to take a long time with lower temperatures initially used than was common in Scotland. This would have added greatly to the oiliness. Gradually, wheat and rye were dropped from the recipe although oats were still in use until the 1960s.

But that changed as well with the incorporation of more unmalted barley. By the time the new Midleton plant swung into operation, oats, like rye and wheat were, from a pot still point of view, a thing of the past. This has meant that the taste of pure pot still Irish whiskey has also changed somewhat over the years; hardly any difference between now and the early 1970s, but by some margin from a century ago.

Midleton not only makes pure pot still but also, when required, a pure single malt, and also grain whiskey from column stills. What is so remarkable is that Midleton makes several styles of each type, be it pot still, pure malt or single grain, and its range of whiskeys cover a wider spectrum than any other distillery I know in the world.

Contents apart, the first stages of the making of all types of whiskey at Midleton, Bushmills and Cooley are identical. First the grain is crushed into a powder containing the husks called "grist". This is then added to hot water, which at Bushmills is 63°C (145°F) and at Midleton a slightly cooler 60°C (140°F), in a metal vessel called the mashtun and then slowly stirred by mechanical means. The natural sugars present in the grist and other solubles dissolve into the water which is then drained off. This process is repeated twice before the spent solids, called "draff", are removed. The water from the third mashing is held back and used with the first water from the next mashing using fresh grist. In other words, the first water of any mashing contains a percentage of water from the previous mash, which goes some way to creating a form of consistency.

The liquid containing the dissolved sugars and grain, called "wort", is then pumped into a set of vessels called washbacks, or at Midleton, the "fermenters". At this point, yeast is added which reacts with the sugars to produce a beer-like liquid, orange-brown in colour at about 8.5 per cent alcohol by volume (abv). When fermentation has run its course and the liquid quietens from a foaming, frothing cauldron to a tranquil, murky lake, it is then pumped through to the stills.

It is at this juncture that things begin to change. At Bushmills the wash is distilled three times in medium-sized pot stills, each time with increasing alcoholic strength as the distillate becomes lighter in density. At Cooley the malt is distilled twice, as is the practice amongst most Scottish distilleries, thus producing a slightly heavier spirit. At Midleton, however, the fate awaiting the wash depends on precisely the kind of whiskey they want to produce.

If the wash is to be pumped directly into the large pot stills, it is likely to be a mixture of malted and unmalted barley. Midleton hasn't produced any pure malt whiskey since

February 1991, although during 1997 there is every chance they will distil some more to replenish their stocks.

For pot still whiskey the grist will have been made up from anything within the parameters of 60 per cent unmalted barley and 40 per cent malt, or from a straight 50/50 split. From this range of mixes three types of whiskey can be produced: light pot still; medium/modified (known as Midleton Mod Pot); or heavy. Once they made a fourth, even heavier version called Trad (Traditional) Pot. At any other distillery the results will be achieved in the final part of the process. After all three distillations, the stillman can produce a heavy whiskey by capturing a greater portion of the latter part of the distillate "run" which contains some of the heavier oils. The lighter the spirit he requires, the more central portion of the run will be selected each time. The result is a lighter spirit, and one which is higher in alcoholic strength.

There are other processes to complicate matters. As well as the use of the three pot stills (wash, intermediate and spirit) some of the whiskey is distilled through two column stills designed for the making of grain whiskey. These stills, like most column stills around the world, are pretty boring to look at. But at Midleton they are quite fascinating because they are linked to the pot stills so that some of the impure spirit, called "low wines", which runs off from the wash pot still, is fed through both column stills before being pumped back into the second (intermediate) pot still and then into the final, spirit pot still. In the intermediate still it rejoins the distillate considered to be of the highest quality from the first run from the wash still. Meanwhile in the first column still (the wash column) the impure spirit from the first pot still does not make its long, complicated journey alone: it is mixed with the impure spirit from the intermediate and spirit pot stills.

By the time the mid-cut of the run from the spirit still is filled into cask it will have been distilled at least three times, and a small percentage of it five times. It is the most complicated whiskey-making system in the world. And it is repeated when Midleton Mod Pot is produced, except that the stillman does not select such a narrow band of the mid-cut from all three stills. Only when they produce a heavy pot still whiskey are the column stills dispensed with altogether. With so many different types of pot still whiskey to choose from, the blender is then able to select different styles, at different ages, for different brands.

Midleton also produces the grain whiskey required not only for their own blends but also Bushmills. Sometimes the grain is made from a mixture of malted (20-25 per cent) and unmalted (80-75 per cent) barley. This tends to produce a more fully flavoured grain whiskey than when they use wheat or maize. Originally the distillery used only maize, but it was found to be more economic to convert to wheat, which gives a softer, sometimes spicier taste on maturation. However, in the spring of 1994 Midleton switched back to maize. Although it is more expensive to import, it was considered a more economic proposition when the distillery was working flat out. The great problem with wheat is that there is no husk when it is milled and after mashing it leaves a mess which is time-consuming to clear up. And even in an Irish distillery, time is money.

Column stills, or patent stills as they are also known, are much more efficient than pot stills. They distil continuously, unlike pot stills which must be cleaned out after every use. They also produce a purer, more alcohol-rich product, but like pot stills they are used to distil grain spirit three times. Sadly, their efficiency means they also remove the very oils which go to make pot still whiskey so flavoursome. When required they also make the spirit needed for the company's gin and vodka brands.

One of the great features of the Midleton distillery is the acres upon acres given over to warehousing. In Scotland, warehouses tend to be smaller than at Midleton and the system of stacking or "racking' the casks is also different. Usually in Scotland distillers rack their whisky in long rows side by side. At Midleton the casks are stacked upright on palates which are then placed on top of each other, a process which is much less labour intensive. Theory suggests that the casks will have less air circulating around them and so maturation should be slower. So far this has not been noticeable, and with the climate at Midleton being generally warmer than the Highlands, maturation actually takes place at a slightly faster rate. Irish whiskey is matured more extensively in old sherry casks than in Scotland and the company's recent investment in buying brand new ones from Bodegas in southern Spain has been vast. Also, for the maturation of the pot still whiskey Irish Distillers claim to use the cheaper, ex-bourbon casks for a shorter period than Scottish distillers.

When whiskey matures in ex-sherry casks, the alcohols in the spirit leach out the sherry which has soaked into the wood and, depending on how long it is left to mature, also start working on the chemicals in the wood. When whiskey is filled into old bourbon casks, the bourbon they formerly held has no effect on the whiskey whatsoever. But since these bourbon casks have originally been charred, the spirit is able to find its way into the exposed, fresh wood via the thousands of minuscule cracks which will have appeared. The whiskey starts extracting chemicals from the wood which helps develop its flavour. If it is left too long the flavour of the whiskey suffers and it will take on a very woody, vanilla character.

Old whiskey does not guarantee quality. Part of the art of making whiskey is selecting casks to be used when they are peak condition. In exceptional cases in Scotland that could be after 30 to 40 years. In Ireland it is rarely beyond 20.

But no matter how good all these whiskeys are, be they pot still, single malt or grain, they could all easily be wasted if the final and most important stage is not carried out correctly: the blending. At Bushmills and Cooley the blends are made from a single malt whiskey and grain whiskey. At Midleton, Barry Walsh has a myriad of choices available and the character make-up of every whiskey is determined by a formula of ages and wood-types for every brand. Even the single malts and pure pot still have to be blended in a sense: this is called "vatting" which is the mixing together of whiskeys from the same distillery. In contrast when working with Bushmills malt he knows exactly how much 10-year-old malt whiskey he requires from sherry casks and how much 11-year-old from bourbon casks, and so on.

In Scotland, the constituent whiskies of some blends are "married" together for anything up to six months by dumping the contents of the casks into large troughs and then pumping the whisky into enormous holding vats. The idea is that the many different types of malt and grain then get the chance to fuse or marry. Single malts are sometimes treated similarly to allow the distillate from sherry and bourbon casks to find a level ground. This is not the case in Ireland.

For brands such as Jameson, Power's and Paddy, the casks will be vatted together for two days, perhaps even three. It is only with highly specialized whiskeys like Jameson 1780, Distillery Reserve, Midleton Very Rare and the

incomparable Redbreast that the constituent whiskeys may have been vatted for a full month before bottling.

But you should always remember this: no matter what the back of any bottle tells you, whiskeys never remain exactly the same – it is simply impossible. The marketing people in Scotland and Ireland may want you to think that, but the people involved in the day to day making of whiskey know better. Whiskeys mature slightly differently in different casks; temperatures of warehouses fluctuate over the seasons and there .might be a slight variance in the malt used or the time taken to distil and so on. Whiskeys all have unmistakable characters, but they are never exactly the same. So although a vatting for Hewitts may be exactly identical each time in terms of the choice of wood, the age of the malts and grains chosen, a vatting made six months afterwards may be a tad sweeter, a fraction maltier, a degree spicier.

This, in essence, is the most fascinating of mysteries which makes Irish whiskey so special.

Right
*A is for Allman's
– a now defunct
brand from the
north of the
island.*

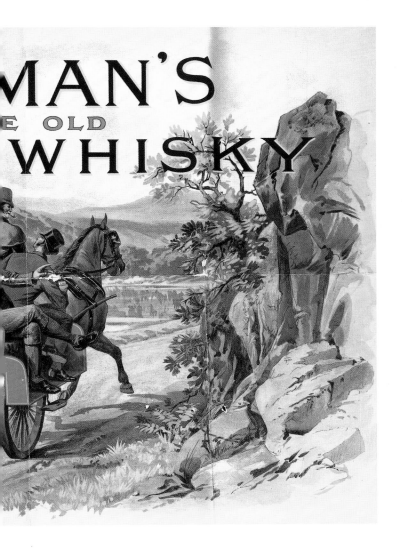

CHAPTER FOUR

AN A-Z OF DISTILLERIES & BRANDS

*All whiskeys are 40 per cent alcohol by volume (abv)
unless otherwise stated.*

AVOCA

A whiskey which didn't even exist when my last book was written in 1994 and already this has become a near extinct Irish species. Named after a

TASTING NOTES AVOCA

NOSE Young, sweet-ish malt, some vanilla but infested with massive grain character, and quite dry at that.

TASTE Quite fatty on the palate and initially to start but it is the grain which is coming through in force. What little malt character there is arrives for the middle but is quickly blasted aside by the drying re-emergence of the grain.

FINISH The grains carry on their own merry way. There is the arrival of some toffee sweetness from the wood but the grain ploughs its lonely, dry furrow.

COMMENTS An Irish with limited complexity. This is more similar to a single grain whiskey in character than it is a blend. But such is the fine quality of Cooley's grain whiskey it makes for a light and, it has to be said, pleasant whiskey. But certainly not a classic.

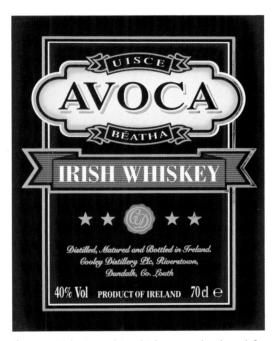

famous Irish river, this whiskey was developed for Dunne's Stores, one of the nation's institutions. Despite being four years of age and a very small proportion of sherry wood added, it has not been a whiskey to set the world alight and has now been discontinued from Dunne's shelves. By way of compensation it has found its way into the Czech Republic and there are efforts to introduce it to Spain. An attempt to find a Dutch market initially floundered: they felt it sounded more like their own drink advocaat! However, it has arrived there at last, but under the title of Finnegan.

BALLYGEARY

A brand-new whiskey, launched in the build up to Christmas 1996. With both malt and grain being distilled at Cooley it has been blended by Invergordon, a Scottish distiller which specializes in a light style. The closest relative is probably the Waitrose own label. An impressive distribution is assured in the United Kingdom by the brand being part of the Malt House Vintners range. This is the wines and spirits division of the successful Bookers Cash and Carry chain. As a result, the whiskey is likely to be found in corner shops and off licences throughout the UK. There is no past-known Irish whiskey by this name: it was invented by Malt House Vintners specifically for their spirit range.

TASTING NOTES BALLYGEARY

NOSE The tell-tale signs of Cooley's grain is here with aplomb. There is a firmness and an un-severe dryness which is always attractive but this is sweetened very subtly by the malt. No more than a touch of oak – a little divergence to an otherwise light and uncomplex nose.

TASTE Despite the nose the first thing to hit home here is the dryness. There is a certain fatness which is badly needed to give the whiskey some substance and when the toffee caramel creaminess subsides the grain picks up with beautifully defined vanilla.

FINISH Medium to long and light. We are now down to the wood effect on the grain whiskey as the malt has all but vanished. Some dark chocolate comes into play here, always a good sign. A few final, teasing peppery notes, but nothing too violent.

COMMENTS A simple whiskey, not a million miles away in character from Erin Isle and closer still to Waitrose. Although sweet on the nose with the malt more evident, this doesn't translate on the palate where it is detectably lighter. This is a light whiskey, young in character. The delicious dark chocolate finish is closer to a whiskey twice its age. Never a world-beater but an honest, enjoyable dram.

BUENA VISTA

When American journalist Stanton Delaplane stopped off at Shannon Airport on the west coast of Ireland on a return journey home, the bartender who prepared him an Irish Coffee to keep out the cold had little idea that he was to become a trendsetter. Delaplane was so impressed with this comforting concoction that he passed on the recipe to the bartender at his downtown haunt, the Buena Vista Cafe, in San Francisco.

That was in 1952 and over 40 years later no other place in the whole of America turns out Irish

Coffee in the quantity of the now famous California cafe at Fisherman's Wharf. To cope with demand the management of Buena Vista struck a deal with Irish Distillers soon after 1966 to supply an Irish whiskey to their own requirements. Transatlantic traffic now amounts to some 3,000 cases a year. It is the only

TASTING NOTES BUENA VISTA

NOSE Despite the grain which springs to the fore, there is an almost sophisticated pot still weightiness which also adds a distinct, honeyed sweetness.

TASTE Very soft and honeyed to start, in fact, very enjoyable and relaxing with the pot still holding sway in the beginning.

FINISH Quite long with the malt dissipating early on to be replaced by a bitter, but never overly-bitter graininess coupled with a chocolate-fudge creaminess. In there somewhere a spiciness thinks about taking off, changes its mind, and never leaves the ground.

COMMENTS This is supposed to be a near relation to Tullamore Dew. A comparative tasting shows Buena Vista has considerably more elegance and is not so constrained by the rigidity of the grain. They are closely related, but Buena Vista – although by no means the perfect whiskey for those looking for a powerful, traditional, pot still Irish character – reveals that there is a fine line between where grain dominates at the cost of all else, and where it is just held in check. Always serve at warm room temperature and never cool or serve with ice when the grain ruins it. Perfect for the Californian climate.

blended whiskey supplied on an exclusive basis by Irish distillers to anyone in the world.

As it was designed for Irish Coffee, like Dunphys and Murphys which were sold in the States for the same purpose, it is extremely light in character; a close relation to Tullamore Dew in style but a tad heavier on the malt and pot still. It is for sale only at the Buena Vista Cafe, but if you don't want it in your coffee, $18.75 enables you to take a bottle home for a closer inspection.

BUSHMILLS DISTILLERY

Anyone shipwrecked in the North Channel between Kintyre and Ireland will be confused if, after tramping across land looking for habitation, they come upon the proud twin pagodas of Bushmills Distillery. It looks more like a Scottish distillery than many found in the Highlands. Its lines are classically those of distilleries built in the boom years of Scotch whisky in the late 19th century, and are on a very grand scale.

But Bushmills is not only Irish, it is Ulster's final bastion of whiskey production. When the distillery was destroyed by fire in 1885 it was hardly surprising that the reconstructed distillery would not look out of place on Speyside or Islay. The owners started again with state of the art design and technology and some of the specialists brought in were, indeed, from Scotland.

The history of "Old Bushmills" begins, however, long before that great fire of November 25, 1885. Every bottle of Bushmills currently sold

Opposite
A turn-of-the-century showcard for "old" Bushmills depicting the "new" distillery which had recently been rebuilt after a fire in 1885.

today, irrespective of the brand, will tell you that its contents come "From the World's Oldest Whiskey Distillery". The claim is based on the undisputed fact that on April 20, 1608 a licence was granted by Sir A Chichester, the Chief Governor of Ireland to Sir Thomas Phillipps, King James I's Deputy for the Plantation of Ulster "for the next seaven yeres, within the countie of Colrane, otherwise called O Cahanes countrey, or within the territorie called the Rowte, in Co. Antrim, by himselfe or his servauntes, to make, drawe, and distil such and soe great quantities of aquavite, usquabagh and aqua composita, as he or his assignes shall thinke fitt; and the same to sell, vent, and dispose of to any persons, yeeldinge yerelie the somme 13s 4d..."

What is also beyond doubt is the simple fact that the Bushmills Old Distillery Company was not formed for another 175 years by a Hugh Anderson. When, in 1891, the company advertised their new pure malt whiskey, Old Glynn Bush, they proudly displayed 1784 as their year of establishment and, for many years after, moulded that date on every bottle produced. Bushmills's marketing people may have forcibly argued that although the present distillery was not operational until **that date**, the licence gives them every right to claim to be the oldest distillery in the world. This is a view I have never subscribed to and even by their own strange method of measuring they are wrong. Similar seven-year licenses to distil were granted all over Ireland

during the same period. There was one dated, March 23 1608 granted to George Sexton (gent) for seven years, for the province of Leinster; rent five Irish shillings. That area covers Co. Louth where the rival Cooley distillery is now situated, so that distillery (built in 1989) pre-dates Bushmills (built in 1784) by a month!

However, on January 10, 1608 another gentleman, Charles Waterhouse, had already been granted a licence to distil for the whole province of Munster at a rent of 6s 8d Irish, also for seven years. That licence, as it happens, covers the exact spot where the Midleton Distillery today stands which means that every bottle of whiskey currently produced in Ireland, be it by the giant Irish Distillers company or little Cooley, has exactly the same right as Bushmills to date itself 1608. Meanwhile Paddy, Power's and Jameson, the famous fruits of Midleton, could usurp their sister distillery and claim instead to be made at the oldest distillery in the world. Except, of course, they weren't. The Midleton distillery originally dates back to 1825 and was rebuilt in the 1970s. So, at the end of all that, one thing is crystal clear: Bushmills is easily and indisputably the oldest distillery in all Ireland, not the world, and should be sufficiently proud of that alone, not to mention the quality of some of the great whiskey it makes.

That claim is further strengthened by evidence that illegal distillation had been carried out on the Bushmills site since at least 1743, and with little wonder. The area in which the distillery and the village-cum-town of Bushmills is situated was known as "The Route" on account of the River Bush being forded there by the road running from the ancient Irish capital of Tara to Antrim. For that reason any illicit whiskey found a market from both locals and passing trade. Also, nearby was a copious supply of peat and, next to where the distillery is located, a stream called St Columb's Rill (so named since it was a favourite haunt of that Saint as a boy) which empties its sweet, slightly peaty water into the Bush. Then, as now, the water was perfect for the making of whiskey.

The legalized Bushmills Distillery, like so many in Ireland at that time, was not an immediate success. Not only had it to contend with illicit distillers but five other licensed distilleries located in the area. It also needed to sell its wares in America and the West Indies to survive. For long periods it was forced to close and when a census of operating distilleries in all Ireland was conducted in 1821, Bushmills, which by this time had passed through not only Anderson's hands, but those of several others, was not amongst them.

When Alfred Barnard visited Bushmills, as part of his pilgrimage around Britain's distilleries in 1885/6, things had changed for the better. Annual output was a healthy 100,000 gallons; they had formed an arrangement with local farmers to produce the barley they needed; the whiskey was conveyed by the novel means of an electric railway from Bushmills to Portrush, six miles away, from where it was shipped to its markets all over the world. They had even set up a head office in Belfast, complete with sampling and board rooms.

At that time Bushmills did not make pure malt whiskey. It made pure Irish pot still, using a mixture of malted and unmalted barley. It was probably not until they launched the Old Glynn Bush in 1891 that they tentatively entered a market which they would later dominate. Evidence suggests they first made pure malt in 1887 in order to launch a special bottling to mark Queen Victoria's Diamond Jubilee 10 years later, of which 10,000 cases were produced. A wait of about four years before bringing Old Glynn Bush into the world sounds about right. It is possible that the distillery became all-malt when it was rebuilt in 1885, making Old Glynn a smoother 6-year-old. For reasons you will discover, we shall never know for certain.

The turning point of the company's fortunes had been the buying of the distillery on August 20, 1860 for £500 by Ballymoney spirit merchant James McColgan and one Patrick Corrigan, who died five years later. With Corrigan's widow, Ellen, McColgan set about securing the future of a distillery which was lucky to have survived through a prolonged period of poor trading. In 1880 they formed the distillery into a limited liability company. Under his leadership its fame grew around the world and the first of a number of gold medals were won at exhibitions in Europe, the USA, Australia and South Africa.

Opposite
A Bushmills showcard takes pride of place in a local pub window.

Even so, the distillery had a chequered career. In 1891 the company was reformed with the Mayor of Belfast, Charles Connor, and James Boyd taking control, but by 1895 it was in liquidation. It was reformed in August 1896, this time as The Old Bushmills Distillery Co. Ltd, the name it still carries. By 1921 the company was again in the hands of the receivers.

It took the wily business know-how of another Boyd, almost certainly unrelated, to finally get the company not only up and running again, but set on a course for long-term success. He was a remarkable man by the name of Samuel Boyd, a Belfast wine and spirit merchant. He had been operating since before the First World War and was wealthy enough to buy Old Bushmills when it became available again in about 1923. It was seven years, though, before he registered it as a limited liability company, by which time the distillery was

in sound condition. Oddly, Old Bushmills had been saved by not only a devout Presbyterian, but also by a man who was not beyond writing temperance pamphlets despite the fact his vast wealth had been borne on the back of alcohol. Boyd died in 1932 and the distillery continued to prosper in his family's hands and was conveniently helped by the Repeal of Prohibition in America the following year.

Expansion followed which also meant acquisition and in 1933 they bought Ireland's original malt distillery, Coleraine, and in 1936, a second, much smaller, distillery in the same town, Killowen. In 1941, fate at last caught up with the charmed life of the company records which had survived the all-consuming fire of 1885 having just been moved to the new Belfast headquarters. During one of the numerous raids on Belfast docks by German bombers, the Hill Street offices took a direct hit and all the company's documents and painstakingly detailed ledgers were lost. Fortunately, no lives were and Old Bushmills carried on regardless, despite the fact a lot of whiskey, as well as the bottling plant, had also been lost in spectacular fashion when the Gordon Street bonds were ablaze.

Wars meant shortages, and the shortage of whiskey meant that although post-war trading would be difficult and funds were low, existing stocks were worth their weight in gold. It left the company ripe for takeover, and this followed in 1946 when Isaac Wolfson, the textile magnate who owned Great Universal Stores, took control. He allowed the Boyds, with their knowledge of the business, to continue to run the show as Wolfson used his financial clout to establish Bushmills in countries of which the Boyds had only dreamed.

In 1964 the ownership changed hands again. This time the move made even better commercial sense. Great Universal had not otherwise been involved in the drinks trade, but the new masters, Charrington, were long-established. With the London-based brewers owning 5,000 pubs and 650 off-licences, the distillery had a captive market. One of their first moves was to bring all the bottling from Coleraine to Bushmills and develop a new blending area. The distillery was becoming self-sufficient.

By the time the last of the Boyds had retired from
the Bushmills board in 1973, the distillery had
again changed hands. Once more the step was in
an upward direction with Canadian distillers
Seagram buying control. Bushmills had remained
the last distillery in Ireland to stay outside the Irish
Distillers Group when that was formed in 1966.
Irish Distillers bought Bushmills shares from
Seagram and the result was that by 1972 IDG
finally achieved overall control. And with the
parent company being eventually taken over by
Paris-based Pernod-Ricard, not only was the
opportunity for Bushmills to further
establish itself worldwide greatly
enhanced, but the long-term future of the
distillery finally secured beyond doubt.

5-YEAR-OLD SINGLE MALT

This is the youngest single whiskey bottled
by Bushmills exclusively for the Italian
whiskey drinker who for whatever reason,
appears to enjoy youthful whiskey. The
biggest whisky success story in Italy has
been the Glen Grant 5-year-old Scotch
malt and the Bushmills 5-year-old has
been designed to attack the same market.
The brand has been in Italian outlets since
1992. But because Bushmills Distillery
does produce a rather light whiskey there
are more sherry casks used in this vatting
than the 10-year-old which is established
on the market.

TASTING NOTES BUSHMILLS 5-YEAR-OLD SINGLE MALT

NOSE Raw, citrussy and youthful. The malt is very clean indeed, but it is really light.

TASTE Quite fat on the mouth, oily and very beautifully malty. There is an unmistakably sweet maltiness which sets Bushmills apart from everything else at any age, and it is here in abundance.

FINISH Piles of vanilla and all things bourbon cask, including chocolate and spice. Some very shy sherry notes also float about at the finish.

COMMENTS A quite different character to the Glen Grant which originally set the 5-year-old trend in Italy since this is softer and oilier. For its tender age, though, it does have a surprising depth, and it is surprisingly enjoyable. I didn't expect this. I have been able to taste this at cask strength before being reduced and it is then absolutely superb. They really should think about releasing that, also!

10-YEAR-OLD SINGLE MALT

During the long hot summer of 1984, Bushmills Distillery unwittingly turned full circle. It had just launched its first pure malt whiskey since the Second World War and it was approaching its centenary since changing codes from a pot still to an all-malt distillery.

Bushmills 10-year-old was first offered to the home Irish market but since then its exposure has grown considerably. Now commonly found on supermarket shelves throughout the United Kingdom, it is accepted as one of the most recognised faces of Irish whiskey. In 1993 it was introduced into the USA for the first time where Original Bushmills, or White Bush, had been a favourite for many years.

TASTING NOTES Bushmills 10-year-old Single Malt

NOSE Rather too light and spirity when cold but once warmed in the hand, whilst remaining light, it becomes an altogether maltier whiskey with a hint of sherry. Oddly, despite being all malt, it does have a pot still brittleness to it which gives it a discernibly Irish edge.

TASTE A sweet start with even a gentle fruitiness. But the middle is emphatically malt and the sweet richness, helped out by some sherry cask, is gradually replaced by a more austere dryness.

FINISH Quite long with lots of malt and toffee and a pleasant spiciness. A chocolate-vanilla feel from the use of ex-bourbon casks makes for a dry finish with a rumbling bitterness in the background.

COMMENTS This is a very pleasant malt: simple, untaxing and slightly fuller-bodied than of old. It is also a rather lazy malt which resists asserting itself on the tastebuds as its original bright start suggests it might. Very refreshing, quaffable and moreish.

The whiskeys used in the vatting of this single malt range from 10 to 12 years, with the occasional batch of 13-year-old casks being added for good measure. Being a light malt, only a little new sherry wood is used in maturation, but certainly enough to give it a fruity feel.

BUSHMILLS DISTILLERY RESERVE

Following the success of the Jameson Distillery Reserve – available only to those ardent whiskey connoisseurs making the pilgrimage to Midleton – Bushmills felt duty-bound to follow suite. Launched in early 1996 this was the oldest Bushmills single malt to be made commercially available until the later development and production of the 16-year-old.

TASTING NOTES

NOSE Pretty striking for a Bushmills. The 10-year-old is flat and uninspiring. An extra few years and some judicious use of sherry cask makes an enormous difference. Should be popular among Canadian tourists. They like almond soap, and there is that kind of character to sit alongside the vanilla and balancing sherry. Really enjoyable. And dry.

TASTE Fuller, fatter, oilier start than one would ever believe from this distillery. Despite this it is a dry beginning with an immediate build up of spices. A toffee-nut sweetness develops with dark cherry. Highly impressive.

FINISH The finish reverts back to its drier beginnings, though this time there is the first real evidence of age with oak and vanilla making its entrance. A sweetness resumes with a top-rate build up of malt, more nutty character and some cream toffee.

COMMENTS You only have to taste this to see why Bushmills are giving such serious consideration to turning their plain Jane 10-year-old into something a little older. Some excellent sherry casks have been used in the making of this and its doubtful that such a high standard could be kept for a mass-marketed malt. Whatever, should you ever be at the distillery you would be missing a treat if you ignored this magnificent dram.

BUSHMILLS DISTILLER'S RESERVE

Enjoying the increasing demand for Irish whiskey, Bushmills decided to set up an entirely new concept for the genre: single cask, cask-strength bottlings in the name of individual customers. Bottled under a special, classy green label with the name of the customer clearly marked, the bottles are packed in neat wooden boxes, some bearing exclusive name plates. One glitch is that the labels give the cask's number but not the year of distillation or bottling so the person considering buying it has no way of knowing the whiskey's age. (Apart from reading this book, of course!) So far there have been four casks used: the first two were Allders Duty Free for their Whiskies of the World shop at Heathrow and the other was the more local Downtown Radio station. Another, a 9-year-old 2nd fill sherry hogshead, cask number 2328 (distilled February 25, 1986, bottled June 1996), has been split among different buyers and bottles are likely to find themselves coming up in auction over the next decade as collectors' items. They cost anything between £35 and £100, depending on which kind of packaging the customer requires. At the time of going to press only 44 of the available 306 bottles are accounted for: numbers 1 to 40 have been taken up by Coca Cola Northern Ireland; number 41 is in the possession of Jameson director Francesco Taddonio and numbers 43-44 have been acquired by Ulster Television. As for number 42: that's mine! Others are certainly going to follow.

TASTING NOTES BUSHMILLS DISTILLER'S RESERVE CASK 2328

NOSE A sultana-sweetness is kept in check by some striding malt. There are some oaky vanillas and a soft spirity kick. But all this is finely balanced with the malt, hints of butterscotch and ultra-delicate sherry. Charming.

TASTE The maltiness from the very start is almost overwhelming. The spirit evident on the nose turns up powerfully but rather than being rough and exhausting carries with it some toffee-raisin sweetness and barley juice. The middle is quite stunning with the malt now even more vivid and assertive. This is something very big, indeed with a brittle hardness one would normally associate more with Midleton pot still than Bushmills malt.

FINISH Does it end? It does, eventually, but you have to wait a minute or two. In the meantime sit back and wallow in the malty theme. The sherry returns but without conviction and the soft oaks are quite startling. This shows itself by a powerful fly-past of chocolate and cocoa plus vanilla.

COMMENTS An entirely different animal to the other Distillery Reserve bottlings and a clue to its character is given by the relatively light colour of the whiskey. Here the sherry takes a back seat and has to be found rather than presenting itself. This is, by far, the maltiest Irish whiskey I have ever discovered. Irish Distillers won't thank me for saying this, but it is so far removed from a standard Bushmills 10-year-old you have to pinch yourself to believe they are related. Brilliant.

DOWNTOWN RADIO

Launched in March 16, 1996 as a limited edition for one of Northern Ireland's commercial radio stations to mark their 20th anniversary. Just a single cask numbered 12488 was used and bottled at 60 per cent abv with a healthy accent put on sherry with second fill cask being selected. What the bottle doesn't tell you is that the whiskey was distilled December 4, 1987 and bottled in February 1996, making this an 8-year-old – the only time I have known a single malt whiskey from this distillery to be marketed at such an age. Restricted to 331 bottles.

TASTING NOTES DOWNTOWN RADIO

NOSE The sherry strikes out confidently and its purposeful character adds unmistakable Oloroso to the amazingly soft malt. A hint of apple and pear adds to the grape.

TASTE That extra touch of sherry gives an uncharacteristic honey-sweet fullness to the start of this whiskey. There are ripe, plumy fruits and a gradual build up of vanilla though a youthful freshness prevents the oak having a very big say at all.

FINISH Delicious cocoa tones battle through despite the sherry notes which hang on until the very last rays disappear.

COMMENTS Bushmills suffers from being just a shade too light. However, this proves that by adding just the right amount of sherry without completely obliterating the youthful malt, a fine balance can be achieved and the whiskey is quite capable of holding weight and richness. One of the finest commercial single malts I have yet tasted.

WHISKIES OF THE WORLD (ALLDERS)

Launched in 1995 two casks, 11756 and 11757, each bottled at cask strength from first-fill sherry, ie: the whiskey inside those barrels was the first to be put into it upon its arrival from Jerez. The casks were filled December 1984; bottling was carried

TASTING NOTES ALLDERS CASK 11756

NOSE Highly pungent sherry clings to every crevice within the glass. Thick and heady, it also enjoys a soft spiciness. The malt just manages to fight through to add a degree of balance but there is a cleanness to the sherry which is truly astounding.

TASTE A whiskey which tastes exactly how it noses. There is a thickness to the sherry which you feel you could stand a spoon in and this is perfectly complimented by a dry, peppery spiciness which guarantees the sherry is not entirely overwhelming. Very fat in the mouth with enormous presence and a fine sweet malt adding sufficient counterbalance, though only just.

FINISH The spice continues to tingle, while the dry sherry notes slowly and reluctantly fade. This is an elegant dryness. The oak arrives only at the very end as the dryness intensifies; good bitter cocoa fights through at the very death.

COMMENTS For those who prefer a sherry-influenced whisk(e)y this is an absolute must. Some sherry bottlings of various malts in Scotland have tried to emulate the success of Macallan, often with disastrous effects. This is quite different from a Macallan in that the malty sweetness hangs on here by just a thread and if it was lost would be a disappointment. This whiskey has a surprising delicacy and the peppery notes are a delight. Highly impressive stuff, indeed.

TASTING NOTES Allders Cask 11757

NOSE The sweet pungency of the Oloroso leaps at you three dimensionally. For best effects, oxidize in the glass for five to 10 minutes and nose when room warm when the raw sherry has shifted shape and there is a mixture of softer prunes and juicy fresh dates.

TASTE Big, roasty start, dry and sherry assertive. This is enormous whiskey, but Bushmills being such a light malt, and this sherry being so clean and fresh, it is the wine which dominates. There are some powering toffee notes in there, not to mention a degree of molasses-rich sweetness which weaves intriguingly with the dry sherry.

FINISH Just a shade fiery with some malt and vanilla finally fighting through. This quietens down after a while to leave some weakened sherry notes to hang on with traces of caramel.

COMMENTS This costs £90 a bottle, so you might be tempted just to apply to the glass by pipette. There is only one way to get the best out of this whiskey and that is to drink it unwatered and with a mouthful. The enormity of the whiskey will hit leaving an indelible impression of Irish single malt whiskey. Although the 11756 and 11757 were filled within seconds of each other, here is an example of how whiskeys can be so different yet have identical backgrounds.

out June 1996, making it an 11-year-old whiskey. The strength of cask 11756 was 58.2 per cent abv while 11757 was 60 per cent abv but reduced to 58.2 per cent. There are 250 bottles of 11756 and 280 bottles of 11757, both Duty Free-friendly 750ml in size, as opposed to the 700ml found in other Distiller's Reserve bottlings. These whiskies are available in the Allders Whiskies of the World outlet in Heathrow's Terminal 1.

16-YEAR-OLD SINGLE MALT

The success of distillers in Scotland, especially Glenmorangie, to produce highly individual and fine quality malts with the use of unusual casks has not gone unnoticed in Ireland. So when it was decided to create a very old Bushmills, this was the opportunity taken to delve into this little-known world of whiskey maturation. Irish Distillers had invested in 100 ruby port pipes from Sandeman. Half were devoted to Bushmills, the remaining 50 were sent to Midleton for experimental work with Jameson- and Power's-style pure pot still. Some half a dozen of the Bushmills pipes have already been used to finish a 16-year-old that they are calling a three wood. This is not a golf club, but a whiskey which has been influenced by three

TASTING NOTES BUSHMILLS 16-YEAR-OLD SINGLE MALT

NOSE Astonishing. There is depth and subtlety here way beyond any other Irish straight single malt on the market. The oak impressively to the fore, but manifests itself not in the usual vanillas or overweight sap that you might expect from a whiskey of this age. There are subtle shades of praline, lemon, orange and marzipan: it's like opening a box of expensive Belgian chocolates or liqueurs. Look deeper still and there you will find the added sweetness of roast chestnuts surrounded by succulent sultanas. Just a sprinkling of warming peppers rounds it off quite nicely.

TASTE A dry yet rich start which enjoys the added bonus of a firecracker explosion of pepper hinted at in the nose. A malt and marzipan sweetness is detectable in the middle but it is a curious, confusing mixture of grapey, winey signals that holds the attention longest. A fine drop.

different types of cask. Despite the 16-year-old tag, some of the whiskey used dates back to 1975. Very early in 1996 a number of casks, evenly split between bourbon and sherry, were vatted together, before being filled into those port pipes. Although first, second and third fill sherry casks had been used, obviously there were very few firsts in order not to entirely swamp any effect the port would have on the maturing whiskey. Not surprisingly, this whiskey has already found its way into duty free, as well as specialist outlets in Ireland, the UK and the USA.

FINISH More of that deep wine, noticeably port this time, and grapeyness clings onto the palate as finally some vanilla and cocoa does arrive to begin a longish, dry finale.

COMMENTS When I first tasted this in 1996 the whiskey had not long been transferred into the port pipe. The result was a gangling, ungainly youth, quite unable to find its feet or show any sign of elegance or charm whatsoever. How a matter of seven months or so can change a picture. At the time I suggested to Barry Walsh that he cut his costs, empty half the port pipes and start again: dauntless, he said he would stand by it and how right he was! As delicious as the whiskey is, it never quite lives up to the nose, though I don't think that would have been possible. This is marvellous Irish, a must for every connoisseur in search of an olive-dry whiskey with remarkable panache and that faint wisp of sweetness which adds the balance.

BUSHMILLS MILLENNIUM MALT

The ultimate Irish whiskey? Perhaps. Those of you with around £5000 to spare will find out in the year 2000 when this 25-year-old whiskey will finally be bottled.

It's not a unique idea since Bushmills's corporate sister distillery in Scotland, Aberlour, is doing

TASTING NOTES BUSHMILLS MILLENNIUM MALT (60 PER CENT ABV, DISTILLED 1975, TASTED 1996)

NOSE Acacia honey lifts the pure malt way above the norm. Highly intense but not so heavy as to blank out the glorious complexity which makes this the finest straight Bushmills I've ever encountered. The oakiness present has begun to give signals normally associated with very young bourbon; there is a hint of ripe orange and freshly ground almond. There is the very faintest echo of grape, but no more than that. Quite lovely.

TASTE The cleanest of malt starts, but on the second wave of taste sensation things really begin to take off. There is a surprisingly deep resonance that is nothing but concentrated malt. The honey tones translate perfectly from the nose with a slab of raisin fudge added for good measure.

FINISH Very long and oily. The oak is beginning to show with hints of toast and liquorice. A dry finish but in perfect harmony.

COMMENTS It is hard to believe we are talking 21-year-old Bushmills here: a decade ago I would have sworn it would not last the pace. When I last tasted it in 1994 the oak was beginning to show through. Now it is there in force, both on the soft bourbon nose and in the finish. There are another three years before it is bottled and it should hang on without the oak becoming too dominant. That apart, I never thought I would taste such a fine whiskey from Bushmills.

something along the same lines. Also an 8- year-old single malt made from purely organic grain will be available by the cask from Springbank, Campbeltown. So Bushmills Millenium is Ireland's contribution.

The casks currently maturing are ex-sherry, but for the last few years before the big day, the whiskey will be finished in bourbon casks so as to make sure the sherry does not dominate too much. Twenty-five years is a long time for a malt as light as Bushmills. Each cask is expected to provide a minimum 250 bottles at 70cl or 228 bottles at 75cl, depending which side of the Atlantic the buyer comes from. The labels will also carry the respective purchaser's name. However it is now entirely sold out.

BUSHMILLS ORIGINAL

No one knows just how long White Bush, as it is affectionately known, has been on the market. Those records were lost when the Bushmills offices were razed in the last war. Equally, there is confusion as to whether it began life as a single malt, or as a blend since Bushmills did not have access to their own grain whiskey until the 1950s. Certainly it is accepted that by the end of the Second World War, it was a blend which did exceptionally

TASTING NOTES BUSHMILLS ORIGINAL

NOSE As has always been the case with this blend, the grain is first on the scene. But now the malt, once a notable absentee, can be spotted behaving quietly along with some tiny but very clean sherry notes. There are also hints of age with some oaky character filtering through.

TASTE The start on the palate is the highlight of this whiskey. It positively bubbles on the palate with the malt, in fruity form matching the grain. The early pleasingly oily sweetness dies off, however, and dark chocolate oaky notes arrive very early.

FINISH The chocolate stays a little while longer as some oiliness remains. However, the grain makes a dark comeback: rather bitter and uncompromising.

COMMENTS Just a couple of years back this was a whiskey I had to be force fed. It was simply too harsh all round. Now some attention has been paid to it: the malt is no longer an outcast and there is a balance which includes favourable amounts of oak. I still think the finish needs something to smooth down those rougher, grainier edges at the very end. But by comparison to how it was as recently as 1994, it has improved just about beyond recognition. The oiliness in particular has helped ensure a richness which makes for a deliciously fine middle, a little reminiscent of chocolate-iced children's party biscuits.

well on the export market. Even today White Bush remains the best known of Bushmills brands and it is the lightest in character bearing the Bushmills name. The malt used in the blending is unlikely to be more than six years old and the grain whiskey only half that age. It has been designed to combat ordinary Scottish blends, so its malt/grain ratio will reflect that, with only about a third consisting of malt. Flatteringly, Irish Distillers have told me that as a direct result of the battering I gave this whiskey in the tasting notes of the first edition, they re-inspected the blend and have remodelled it. Blender Barry Walsh tells me much better and slightly older whiskeys are being used all the time and this up-grading is a continuing process. Obviously a whiskey to watch.

BUSHMILLS BLACK BUSH

As in the case of White Bush, no one has been able to come up with a date of establishment for this most noble of Irish blends. It started life as Bushmills Liqueur Whiskey, designed to be heavy in character to counterbalance the lightness of White Bush. But because of the dark label the customers christened it Black Bush and the name stuck. However, it only enjoyed moderate success in Ireland until the 1960s when a shortage of older stocks of malt meant that it was almost impossible to find in the bars.

A cry went up amongst its regular drinkers and, human nature being what it is, those who hadn't normally drunk it started asking for it and others who had never tasted it wanted to know what all the fuss was about. The rest, as they say, is history.

Bushmills is regarded as the finest blend among drinkers in the north and has a massive following outside Ireland. That is hardly surprising since it has a malt content of around 75 per cent, most of which is 8-years-old with the grain being only a couple of years younger.

TASTING NOTES

NOSE This nose is nothing less than a classic. It has absolutely everything and in the right proportion: exceptionally well-defined malt, gentle sherry notes, high quality grain softness and, dare I say it, a touch of peat in there as well.

TASTE As this whiskey melts in your mouth, you melt into your chair. Very full bodied and malt-rich with a fine sherry background. Again there is a peaty tune being played somewhere and as the malt-sherry middle fades a superb spiciness develops.

FINISH Initially spicy, then dampens down to become sweetish with a pleasant sherry cask/bourbon cask conflict going on between the respective woods. Like the nose and palate, it's never dull and always of the very highest quality.

COMMENTS Some years back I regarded this as probably the finest blend in either Scotland or Ireland. My allegiance has shifted in recent years to Power's, but this is nothing less than a beautifully crafted whiskey which retains a delightful silkiness despite the complexity of all that is going on. An absolute stunner.

Bushmills 1608

This was the first Irish whiskey designed exclusively for the duty free market. Launched in October 1992 the idea was to offer an Irish whiskey with a degree of exclusivity. Even if you visit the distillery, you will not be able to buy it there.

Which is a pity. This is too good a blend for Irish whiskey lovers to miss out on. But the distillers say that they have insufficient stocks of the raw materials required to make this brand to enable them to cater for anything other than the desired duty-free market.

There is hardly any grain in this blend, perhaps around 10 per cent, making it a real top of the range whiskey. The malts used are usually 12 years old although some 14-year-old may sneak in and the grain is a minimum of 12 years old as well. A good cross-section of wood here; a lot of sherry and the ex-bourbon carrying the grain helps give the blend its distinctive spiciness.

Originally this brand was only sold in litre bottles but miniatures are now available. Look for them in your duty-free outlet.

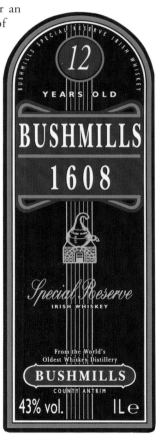

TASTING NOTES BUSHMILLS 1608

NOSE The moment you put a glass of 1608 to your nose, you know you are in the company of a cracker. Malt, sherry and spice all come together in equal measure, each intermingling in a truly astonishing complexity. There are even the faintest traces of pine, mint and honey.

TASTE The palate is immediately held in the grip of a spicy attack which takes you by surprise. Acting as a buffer is a silky honey-rich maltiness with clean sherry notes also adding to the fun. The sum total is a massive assertiveness in the mouth.

FINISH Perhaps the only disappointment with this blend. It dies away rather too quickly, some caramel notes being left behind. So, too, are gentle spices. Maybe a shade too bitter and metallic on the grand finale, though.

COMMENTS One of Ireland's best whiskeys with a complex dovetailing of a great many features on the nose and palate. A very confident whiskey with one of the most luxurious mouth-feels of any whiskey in the world. Beautiful.

***Right**
An old
Bushmills sign
which hasn't
aged quite as
well, under the
drizzling
Antrim skies, as
some of their
world-renowned
whiskeys.*

CASINO

The Paris-based spirit suppliers La Martiniquaise supply own label Irish whiskey to five different large French supermarket chains. The whiskey is produced and blended by Cooley and tankered out in bulk across the Channel. Therefore, despite there being five different brands available in France with impressively colourful labels, the whiskey is, in fact, entirely the same. Casino originally called their whiskey Ken Lough, a brand name which has now been discontinued. Meanwhile Leader Price sell their whiskey as Galoway; Auchan's is called Highfield; Le Clerc is Green Field and Dunlow is the preferred name for the Promodes chain.

TASTING NOTES CASINO

NOSE A slightly unusual Cooley blend with a soft, salty tang to the nose and some firm, young, grassy malt to add attractive richness to the very clean grain.

TASTE After the initial oily softness of the grain comes into play the malt takes up the dominant role and holds its ground firmly. Some attractive bitter-sweet notes make for an acceptable complexity.

FINISH Hints of cocoa and vanilla and just a shade of toffee.

COMMENT It may be light but the malt is impressive here. The simplicity of the whiskey should appeal to many drinkers.

CASSIDY

Above

Green Field and Dunlow – two of the five labels Cooley's Casino brand is sold under in France.

Another Cooley-distilled brand this time exclusively blended for Marks and Spencer worldwide. The first bottlings were made in September 1996 in time for an October launch. A little sherry cask has been used to add a degree of extra body. Marks and Spencer had already enjoyed some success with their own-label Scotch brands, like Kenmore, blended for them by Burn Stewart. This gave M&S spirits buyer Jon Palmer confidence to look for a blend of his own favourite tipple, Irish. His instructions to Cooley were to create something that lovers of Black Bush might appreciate. Samples were tasted blind by members of staff, including those working in the warehouse. Comments were favourable; some, legend has it, thought it was Black Bush they were drinking.

TASTING NOTES

NOSE Finely weighted with caramel and chunky malt. Slightly citrusy in the grand Cooley style but, as ever is the case with the nose of their blends, quite seductive.

TASTE Superb start on the palate with a delicious viscousness holding together a very vivid maltiness. The malt really is the superstar here, though, showing depths that are at first grassy and then biscuity. The grain arrives to form a rich complexity with honey-treacle traces.

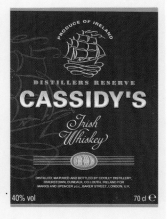

FINISH Long, deep, rich and pretty sophisticated. There is a feeling of just having eaten a slightly toasty curl biscuit that has just been dunked in coffee.

COMMENTS Alongside Kilbeggan and Inishowen this is probably the best blend produced by Cooley. For once they have forsaken the super-light route and added depth and richness. The nose suggests that caramel, used to ensure a colour uniformity, might just have played a small part in this. Whatever the reason, this is a hellish enjoyable Irish whiskey. One which I am sure most people will have difficulty saying no to if offered a refill.

Place the two whiskeys side by side, though, and you would soon taste the difference. Perhaps the only surprise is that given the country from which this whiskey comes, M&S weren't tempted to call it St. Michael!

Opposite
An old
Coleraine
Whisky
showcard depicts
exhibition
medals as well
as the local
attractions of
the Salmon
Leap and
Giant's
Causeway to
enhance
its image.

COLERAINE DISTILLERY

While Bushmills is today known the world over for its single malt Irish whiskey, a century ago it was Coleraine which enjoyed that honour. Only the Waterside Distillery in Derry also made pure malt and although its output was twice that of Coleraine, it was held in only half the esteem. Today Coleraine is just one of a number of Irish distilleries of which little is left intact, having been bought out, swallowed up and then closed. The building apparently began life as a flour mill, which may account for the murals of sheaves which can still be seen woven into part of the remaining structure, but was not converted into a distillery until 1820. While many distilleries struggled to keep going at this time, there was no such problem for Coleraine. By 1845 it was already on sale in the bars of the House of Commons and because of this honour the distillers marketed their malt as Old Irish HC Whisky (always without the "e").

The man who originally supplied it was James Moore who had bought the distillery some time earlier. Moore was a proven distiller, already owning Bann Distillery, and a maltman to boot, so the company was quite well established by the time Robert Taylor, a local dignitary, acquired the distillery in 1869 following Moore's death. It was both rather fitting and also ironic that the distillery bearing the HC logo should pass into the Taylor family's hands, because five years later his brother Daniel became Liberal MP for Coleraine –

and a noted sympathiser of the Temperance movement. Robert Taylor, who had been a partner in his family's grocery business, showed he was not taking his new profession lightly.

As well as the distillery he also ensured that he secured all the stocks of Coleraine whiskey held in bond not only at the distillery but also in Belfast and Ballymena. The reputation of the distillery continued, like its business, to flourish. Between them Taylor and distillery manager Edward Reid made not only one of the most prized malts in Britain, but did so in a distillery which amazed all those who visited it. Among them was Alfred Barnard, coming to the end of his tour of Ireland, who was unusually moved to remark: "In all our wanderings through Erin's Green Isle, for cleanliness, order and regularity, we have seen no

distillery to beat this. The Stillmen seem to take a pride and delight in their work and regard these old Pot Stills with veneration." Oddly, in an age when distillers and brewers set out to collect as many gold medals as they could at Exhibitions, Coleraine was laid back about collecting gongs: it felt confident enough about its product.

The only one it did enter was the Edinburgh Exhibition in 1886. It won! In 1899 Robert Taylor was knighted. He had long been a JP and legend has it, once, when he had the one-legged "Stamper" Thompson up before him on a charge of being drunk and disorderly "Stamper", well known locally as something of a poet, rasped in reply to how he pleaded: "Vance Macauley grew the barley, Robert Taylor brewed the Malt, Stamper Thompson drank the whiskey, So who the devil is at fault?" After Robert Taylor's death in 1902, the distillery fell into decline. It had been taken over by his nephew, Andrew Clarke, but under his auspices Coleraine failed to maintain the high standing it had gained under his uncle's reign. Production ceased in the early 1920s and the distillery remained silent until the late 30s, by which time it had been bought by the Boyds, owners of Bushmills. Although the purchase was made in 1933, it wasn't until 1938 that the Boyds began making malt whiskey there again. But the stills hissed for only a short time before the Second

Above
An old advertisement for Coleraine whisky. – "invariably recommended as the best and safest stimulant."
Opposite
An early 20th-century Coleraine label.

World War and the shortages of barley that brought meant it had to close down again. When peace was won, Coleraine again reopened its doors, not only as a distillery but also as the bottling hall for both distilleries. With the move towards blended whiskey Coleraine was also selected as the distillery to house patent stills to produce grain whiskey alongside its famous malt. But with cost-cutting in operation in March 1964, just two months before Great Universal Stores sold the Bushmills Company to Charrington, and with it Coleraine, the last-ever malt whiskey from this most famous of distilleries was squeezed from the stills. It continued until 1978 as a grain plant but then that arm of the operation was closed down since a similar style grain was by then being produced at Midleton. Found right in the town centre, parts of the old distillery can still be seen today (the warehouses are being demolished as I write), though a block of flats and a nightclub stand on the greater part of the site. To the last, the quality of Coleraine pure single malt whiskey remained wonderfully high. Its closure was a sad loss, not only for distilling in Ulster, but for the Irish whiskey industry in general.

COLERAINE BLEND

The most parochial of all Bushmills whiskeys, this one keeps its fans happy in the northernmost part of Ulster. Only 10,000 cases are produced each year, but that may begin to rise if it continues to improve from the mind-numbingly bland whiskey it used to be. Many hotels and bars I've visited have a bottle around somewhere and its very light style also appears in the outlets alongside other cheaper blends. Launched to keep the old distillery name alive, it barely does justice to it although I've always understood there to be roughly equal portions of grain to malt. Just like White Bush the malt used has been aged about six years and the grain is somewhere around four. It is virtually impossible to find outside Ulster.

TASTING NOTES COLERAINE BLEND

NOSE Uncompromising grain whiskey dominance, and pretty young grains at that. There is a musty maltiness alongside caramel, but it's all too sweet and murky to make any sense out of it.

TASTE Soft and yielding on the palate, the malt flits across the taste buds rather quickly allowing the grain to dominate. There is also some spice around that hasn't been sensed in previous years.

FINISH Quite an attractive, well balanced and rather moreish finish. The malt returns rather superficially but the grain has very pleasant bourbon wood notes and sweet cream-caramel toffee, all of which adds character.

COMMENTS This whiskey has improved out of all recognition from a few years back. Then it was an unsophisticated and bland whiskey with a redeeming and mystifying Irish pot still fruitiness. More recent bottlings have been considerably better structured with the malt having a far greater say at the expense of a grain which had little going for it. By strange coincidence, the introduction of the caramel notes, which I've never noticed before, has arrived at the same time as a marked deepening of the whiskey's colour. Can that by in any way be related? Worth trying these days.

COMBER DISTILLERY

It is hard to imagine Northern Ireland having a dozen working distilleries less than 70 years ago. Yet that was the case, and although that was two fewer than the Irish Free State their combined output was twice as much.

In Eire it was the smaller distilleries which withered and died; in Northern Ireland exactly the reverse happened. By 1953 Ulster's three smallest distilleries, Comber, Coleraine and Bushmills, were what was left of a proud distilling tradition. By the end of the year the number was down to two. The demise of Comber in the February of Coronation year was a sad landmark in Irish distilling history. The silencing of the stills saw the end of the making of pot still whiskey in Ulster: Bushmills and Coleraine made malt or grain only.

The distillery's earliest years were curious. There were two Comber distilleries located in that small town close to Belfast. They were called the Upper and Lower distilleries, and it was the former which was the senior in standing. In some respects the distilleries were twins. Both were established in 1825, though independently, by being converted from buildings serving different purposes.

The Upper Distillery began life as a brewery and malthouse before Johnston and Miller invested the £8,000 required to turn the output from beer to whiskey. Down the road Byrne and Giffikin turned a paper mill into the Lower distillery but some 20 years later John Millar bought out the smaller distillery and ran both simultaneously.

Alfred Barnard did not find either particularly interesting, and obviously having an off day and wearying from his daily grind of measuring all Britain's distilleries to the nearest inch, summed up the two Combers in the briefest terms.

Instead, he found the journey to the distillery much more exciting: "We left the Royal Avenue Hotel in a very tipsy-looking jaunting car, with a driver to match the vehicle. His coat had evidently been handed down from a past generation, its skirts touching his heels, whilst his battered white hat and his knee-breeches were of like ancient date. He assured us on his honour that he would catch the Comber train; he kept his word, but it was at the peril of our lives. He bowled us along almost upsetting us at every corner, we collided with other vehicles, almost ran over one old woman and three street urchins, and we inwardly vowed we would never again let a jarvey know that we were in a hurry."

The Comber Distilleries Company may have been among the first Irish distillers to pioneer bottled whiskey, but the relatively heavy pure pot still they produced began to lose ground in the markets against lighter, blended whiskies. So the company's decline and fall, especially during and after the Second World War, was classic by Irish business standards.

And it sadly reinforced the fact that reputation, of which Comber always enjoyed the very highest, counted for nothing in the harsh climate of modern commerce.

OLD COMBER PURE POT STILL

By the time the Ulster-based wine merchants and distillers agents, James McCabe, managed to get hold of the Comber Distilleries business there was little to salvage.

For 17 years the company had been picked clean, first by H D Wines of Inverness who bought it after its closure. They did a roaring trade out of the scrap and some of the whiskey stocks. In 1957, four years later, two gentlemen called Hollywood and Donnelly bought what remained, sold off even more whiskey and finally, in 1970, McCabe took over. They set about buying up as much old stock of Comber as they could find throughout Ireland's bonded warehouses. But it never amounted to very much. In the early 1980s they launched a brand called Old Comber, bottling the whiskey before the wood did

irreparable damage to it. It was at least 30 years old; less than a few hundred bottles have been sold each year and mainly in Northern Ireland. Stocks are now very low. In fact three years ago I was told by whiskey merchants in the north that the very last drop of Old Comber had long since been drunk. But during the course of researching this book I discovered there are still a couple of hundred bottles in bond. Surely, though, for not very much longer.

TASTING NOTES Old Comber Pure Pot Still

NOSE A glorious and quite unique combination of pure honey and pot still. Very sweet with definite traces of malt with the pot still not being hidden by anything like the amount of wood one would expect from a 30-year-old Irish whiskey. There is an unmistakable resiny presence nonetheless.

TASTE Begins with a soft, breezy maltiness which is attractive for its gentleness. But this is cut rather abruptly short by a wood surge totally out of proportion with the nose. This means the middle is almost non-existent. Yet before the wood arrives one is aware of a strange mint/menthol coolness which combines with an almost cameo pot still appearance.

FINISH Rather disappointing to be honest. The wood takes too firm a grip, with the sappy bitterness refusing to allow the sweet honey tones to get a look in. It does settle down towards the end with that mint/menthol freshness returning and a defiant pot still hardness reminding us, all too briefly, of former glory days.

COMMENTS A truly classic example of a whiskey that has spent too long in the wood. Increasing age does not equal excellence. Despite this it is drinkable, but you are always thinking of how good this might of been at only half its age. If you are lucky enough to spot Old Comber, buy it. This really is one for the collector; and if you must open the bottle then just savour that voluptuously beautiful nose.

CONNEMARA

The so-called traditionalists might throw their hands up at this: Irish whiskey which is peated in a big, big way. Yet, contrary to what has been written in the past, long ago Irish whiskey could often be found to be peaty…just in the same way today that some Scottish single malts are completely unpeated and others have that wonderful, tell-tale turfiness.

Although elsewhere I have devoted a chapter to poteen, the advent of Connemara presents an opportunity to look more closely at just how Irish whiskey was made. For the last 25 years just about every article written about Irish whiskey underlined the belief that peat never played a role in the making of Irish whiskey. Indeed, the argument goes, it was the lack of peat alone that separated Irish from Scotch. That is nonsense, I'm afraid, because it is the grain which sets it apart.

If proof is required, let us inspect the writings of Michael Donovan, Professor of Chemistry to the company of Apothecaries in Ireland. In his *Domestic Economy*, published in 1830, he says of Irish whiskey, "Its peculiar flavour is supposed to be caused by the practice of drying the malt from which it is made by turf. But it does not appear to me that this is the case." After describing a journey he made to a highly regarded illicit distiller, he concludes, "I doubt very much that the flavour of poteen depends on the smoke of turf used under the kiln on which the malt is dried. The distillery told me that his spirit has the same smell and taste on occasion as when coal had been burned under the kiln. His malt had no peculiarity of smell or taste although it often has. I think it probable that these peculiarities depend on the nature of the fermentation, the urging of the distillation so low as to procure, not only the whole spirit, but much of the essential oil. I have found that by making an alcohol perfectly destitute of foreign flavour, dissolving in it a small quantity of essential oil

PURE POT STILL

Connemara,

PEATED SINGLE MALT

40% vol.   70 cl e

Distilled, Matured & Bottled in Ireland. Cooley Distillery Plc, Riverstown, Dundalk, Co. Louth.

IRISH WHISKEY

• PRODUCT OF IRELAND •

from the distiller's faints, and diluting with a little water, a spirit resulted which had very much the flavour of poteen although not precisely. It is possible, however, that the turf smoke with which these mountain distilleries abound may be absorbed by the spirit while running, but most especially by the worts while under fermentation. It is well known that there is a period of the vinous fermentation at which odours are very apt to be absorbed and retained. The steeping [of the malt sacks] in bog water also contributes; for in the subsequent drying on the kiln there may be sufficient odours in some degree to char the bog extract remaining in the malt, thus giving origin to the smell of turf on the spirit".

It is fascinating to note that neither the distiller, apparently an experienced practitioner, nor Donovan, one of the country's leading chemists, recognised the importance peat had upon the character of whiskey in regard to the malting process. This suggests that at that time turf would have been used readily throughout the country wherever it was available. If coal could be obtained more cheaply, that would have been used.

Connemara, so beautifully gilded in peat-reek, is a return to traditional Irish custom. As traditional as using a mixture of malted and unmalted barley.

The first peated whiskey was distilled at Cooley after the stills had first been fired in 1989. However, there were always only very limited stocks but such was the quality of that peated malt it was obvious, from when it was just six months old, that it was destined to become a superstar. I was lucky enough to sample it for the first time around then and suggested they should not waste any of it in a blend, and so far only very small amounts have been spared outside their single malt, though Inishowen benefits from its presence.

Connemara was first suggested as the brand name because distillery manager David Hynes's father, Jack, came from that region and would cut turf himself in his younger days. Some observers reckon the whiskey to be Islay in style; I feel it is a little drier, not in taste, but mouthfeel and displays less of a seaweedy element. It is hard to put into exact words, but there is *something* subtly, almost intangibly, different. A big surprise is the fact that the phenol levels reaches just 15 parts per million compared to 35 ppm for Laphroaig and Coal Ila on Islay and 50 ppm at Lagavulin and Ardbeg.

TASTING NOTES Connemara

NOSE What's this? Irish whiskey and peat? No mistaking: the peat is profound, the smokiness less like an Islay and more like a mainland whiskey with its kippery as opposed to pure iodine quality. There is a heathery floralness and hints of honey. Wondrous.

TASTE Sweet acacia honey and molasses make a glittering impact, but building up degree by degree in oily intensity is that peated malt. By the time it has reached the middle it has consumed almost everything else around, although the maltiness is still able to be detected.

FINISH Like a glorious winter sunset, glorious golden honey notes spread across the mouth with the deep peat rumbling on and on. Some delicious chocolate-vanilla arrives at the finish as some oak gets a word in. But the complexity is mind-blowing. And absolutely mouth-watering.

COMMENTS Genuinely a one-off, being Ireland's only peated malt carries a bit of a burden. But this is stylish, absolutely top rank and near faultless, making light of its youth by showing remarkable maturity. For peat whiskey lovers this is more than a must. Brilliant.

These phenols are diluted even further by something like 20-25 per cent of the malt whiskey used in Connemara being unpeated stuff.

Launched for Christmas 1995, it has spread far and wide, being available in the UK, the Netherlands, Sweden, USA, Denmark and Germany. During 1996, as Chairman of Judges at the 1996 International Spirit Challenge, I had the pleasure of awarding it its first Gold medal (having tasted it blind) and shortly after it received a rare double accolade by achieving Gold at the International Wine and Spirit Competition. Its fame is likely to spread further still.

CONNEMARA CASK STRENGTH

Much of the malt used here was originally distilled in August 1991, the whiskey being vatted in 1996 and returned to cask. Bottled at around 60 per cent abv it was launched in October 1996 and is to be found in speciality whiskey outlets.

TASTING NOTES
CONNEMARA CASK STRENGTH

NOSE This is the unique aroma of peated Irish whiskey as nature intended. When cold, the smokiness is quite lazy; warm in the glass and it starts to lift off into another, medicinal direction and positively amplifies when it reaches the nostrils. Wow!

TASTE Big, fat and oily start with enormous peat surge in the middle. The peatiness is toasty and roasty rather than iodiney. It absolutely fills the mouth yet still enables sufficient malt to come through to give some added complexity.

FINISH Very stark. Massive peat clings to every crevice in the mouth and remains sweet and glorious for three, maybe four minutes.

COMMENTS This is a gentle monster of a whiskey. When the temperature is right it starts off on the nose with the intensity of an active farmyard and totally dominates the palate. In this beautifully natural, undiluted state, this is the most extraordinary whiskey to come out of Ireland in living memory. Top marks for this one, especially in view of its tender years. But for those who cannot negotiate Islay whiskeys, beware.

COOLEY DISTILLERY

Dotted around Ireland are a number of peculiarly-shaped buildings. Designed and constructed in the inter-war years, their only purpose was to turn potato solids and waste into alcohol.

These strange buildings, an early monument to the ugliness created when concrete is combined with steel, are found in the most unlikely places in the Republic. It was the Dublin Government which actually commissioned them to be built and their severity is accentuated by the tranquillity of the settings in which they are found. I accidentally stumbled across one located in a small village not very far from Malin Head, Ireland's most northerly point. It was a near enough replica of the one I had already visited just north of Dundalk whose function in life today is not to distil from potatoes, but from malted barley. For this is now Ireland's third whiskey distillery: Cooley. Considering the short time Cooley Distillery has been in operation it has had a pretty dramatic life. But its gestation was a long affair, going back to the early 1970s when an Irishman studying at Harvard University looked into, as part of his business degree, the marketing of Irish whiskey. As far as John Teeling was concerned, the Irish made the best whiskey in the world but had not the slightest clue how to market it. It was around that time that IDG had taken over Bushmills and were trying desperately to get their product away from the bottom of a marketing trough. Teeling kept his distance from the industry until 1986 when it

became an open secret that Irish Distillers were looking for a major buyer. He hovered around the scene on the off-chance that he could make a successful bid for the company, but in the end it was a larger, international, corporate fish which swallowed the prize. The next step, therefore, was to set up his own distilling company. He had to find other financial partners and when that was achieved he paid the Irish Government £120,000 for the Ceimici Teo Distillery at Dundalk which he immediately renamed Cooley. The buying of the distillery was the easy bit: a further £3,000,000 was spent in turning it into a whiskey distillery complete with pot and patent stills. The distillery also needed some famous names to help sell their new product when it had matured. So they then

Left
An old photograph of the Kilbeggan Distillery. The original home of the Locke and Kilbeggan brands, it is now used by Cooley to house maturing casks.

acquired both the John Locke and Tyrconnell brand names. In 1989 the production of both malt and grain whiskey began. For three years the distillery produced vast amounts of spirit, using the warehouses which once stored whiskey at the old Kilbeggan Distillery and at Tullamore. The arrival of Cooley was seen as nothing less than a commercial annoyance by Irish Distillers since it cut directly across their plan to control the marketing of all whiskey produced in Ireland. By 1992 Cooley was experiencing serious cash flow problems and was looking for a white knight to buy the company. A number of Scottish distillers looked at the business but shook their heads rather than hands. But Irish Distillers could not ignore the 44,000 casks of spirit maturing into Irish

THE
TYRCONNELL
Extra Selected
OLD IRISH WHISKY

Tyrconnell wins!

Andrew A. Watt & Co., Ltd.,
LONDONDERRY.

whiskey which had been stockpiled in those warehouses. Nor the fact that The Tyrconnell Single Malt had been launched onto the market and at least one blend was on its way. Irish Distillers mounted a £22 million takeover bid for Cooley, a move which was welcomed by those who wanted to get some return on the £10 million which had been invested in the project. But an unfair criticism of the quality of Cooley whiskey, backed up by Irish Distillers' known intention of closing the distillery down, meant that those directly involved in its production were keen to keep Cooley if not independent, then certainly out of the hands of Pernod-Ricard, Irish Distillers' owners. Although Irish Distillers actually bought some of Cooley's stocks to help keep the company afloat while the powers that be made up their minds, the takeover was never to go ahead. It was finally scuppered by the Competitions Authority of the Irish Government, even after appeal.

Immediately Cooley went on an international

hunt to find a number of companies willing to underpin the distiller's unstable financial situation. They achieved success in the shape of Borco Marken in Germany, Moet-Hennessy and La Martiniquaise in France and the Kentucky distillers of Heaven Hill in Bardstown who together pushed the Cooley whiskeys in widely differing markets. Also, Cooley went after the own-label and supermarket brand markets, so badly neglected by Irish Distillers, with some considerable success. As a result of these fresh market inroads, the stills, sadly silent during 1994, came back on stream in Autumn 1995 and were still producing fine malt during the fall and early winter of 1996 as I closed this chapter.

Opposite & below

Locke, stock and barrel – Cooley revived the illustrous John Locke brand and found it equally hard to resist having Tyrconnell as a thoroughbred for its stable.

JOHN LOCKE & CO. LTD.
PURE POT STILL
ESTD 1757
AS DISTILLED AT BRUSNA DISTILLERY, KILBEGGAN
WHISKEY

DUNGOURNEY 1964 POT STILL

As a cooper on routine patrol looking for leaking casks tap-tapped his way around old number 11 warehouse at Midleton something very strange happened. He found a cask that was not on the official inventory and that no-one knew anything about. Just every now and again a cask or two of Midleton whiskey from the late, lamented old distillery turns up. And this was one of those magic moments. Many of the very last were used in the first blendings of Midleton Very Rare, though that is no longer the case. Only a matter of a year or two back such a find might not have raised more than faint interest within the company and it is more than likely it would have been dispatched into the vatting tanks holding another vintage of Midleton Very Rare. But because Irish Distillers had discovered, with the obliging aid of an old cask of Coleraine, that there was enormous interest - and profit - in one-off whiskeys from long dead distilleries, they sensibly decided to bottle it as a very rare Irish intact, though giving it the name of the river which runs through the distillery rather than, more fittingly, the distillery itself. I asked manager Barry Crockett if there were possibly any other old gems lying around: "Put it this way, they haven't been found yet." Doubtless a cask or two of Midleton secreted away in a warehouse somewhere in Ireland or abroad may come to the surface and when it does make a point of trying to get hold of it. Those enormous old pot stills made some majestic whiskey.

TASTING NOTES Dungourney 1964 Pot Still

NOSE There is a freshness to the pot still that has no right to be there. But apart from the unmissable unmalted barley there is much more besides: old raincoats after a downpour, a well-worn Winchester; honeysuckle in the rain. Having said that, it's more like a very old Jamaica pot still rum than pot still Irish! Mind-blowing stuff.

TASTE Breath-takingly sweet with honey and molasses to begin and then a malt biscuit with demerara coating. Very fat and full-bodied as you might expect from a whiskey from this distillery.

FINISH The pure pot still doesn't really make itself present until the very end. Yet it is still that molasses theme that follows through. The oak is near non-existent with the exception of just a hint of vanilla and a final, fluffy dryness.

COMMENTS This is masterful stuff, quite a different character to the pre-1960 Old Midleton bottled elsewhere. Yet it still possesses a remarkable Jamaica rum quality, and a classy one at that.

DUNPHYS

Few whiskeys have a more curious history than Dunphys. In effect it was an Irish whiskey to be drunk anything but straight. The 1950s saw Irish whiskey enjoy a mini-boom in the United States for the most unlikely of reasons. A modest craze swept the nation: the drinking of Irish coffee. To fan the flames of this craze it was thought a good idea to produce as cheap an Irish whiskey as possible which people would buy especially for that purpose, while they could keep their better, more expensive brands safely in their cocktail

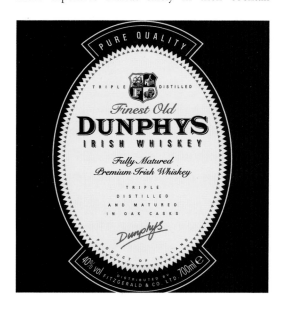

TASTING NOTES Dunphys

NOSE The grain takes solid control here; nowhere near enough malt or pot still balance. Also some odd creosote and tarry notes which spice it up. A hint of sweetness in there, but not enough to create a balance.

TASTE The grain is evident in a somewhat brutal manner, taking no prisoners and making little attempt to charm. Some pot still filters through on the third wave which crashes against the palate, but even this is a rather sorry attempt at achieving some egality.

FINISH Usually, a long finish suggests a classy whiskey. This is the exception: Dunphy is the most bitter and unpleasant of any Irish I can think of. The bitterness seems to go back to that tar and creosote: it's all-consuming and no attractive points manage to battle through. The grain refuses to yield whatsoever.

COMMENTS A terrible disappointment. From the nose through to the finish there is little if any balance or style. The grain is not only dominant, but appears to be of a strain which is quite charmless. Keep it in the coffee cup!

cabinets for more serious drinking. It was decided to create a whiskey which was light in nature, so a blend was produced, made by Cork Distilleries in tandem with some American distillers. To keep the price down further the whiskey was shipped out to the USA in bulk and bottled there. Although the boom, like all fashionable things, peaked and then subsided, Dunphys could still be found in the USA until 1988, when it was withdrawn as part of Irish Distillers' masterplan to concentrate purely on the Jameson and Bushmills brands. But Dunphys lives on in the Irish Republic, a young blend of high grain content fighting it out on the market shelf against the cheaper Scotches.

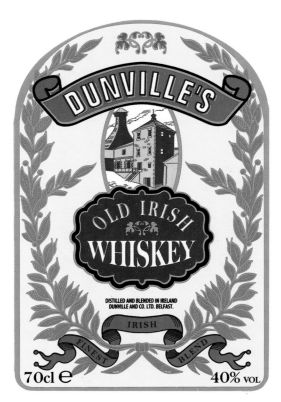

DUNVILLE'S

Dunville whiskey was once a sight as synonymous with Belfast as grey skies and heavy drizzle. Up until a few years ago this great Irish name in whiskey had been forced to become a brand name of a pretty nondescript Scotch whisky. But now the dream of re-uniting the name of Dunville with Irish whiskey has come true with Invergordon

> **TASTING NOTES** Dunville's
>
> **NOSE** Despite its lightness there is a decent fresh maltiness which adds a touch of extra weight than usually found in the lighter Cooley blends. The grain, as ever, is clean and attractive.
>
> **TASTE** A sweet, malty start but this is fleeting as the grain tucks its feet under the table. There is a delicious oiliness which adds a richness you might not expect to be there. Pleasant but uncomplex.
>
> **FINISH** Medium length and predominantly grain. The malt had burnt off just before the middle was reached. This leaves a gentle vanilla and toffee finish which takes the edge off the gradual dryness.
>
> **COMMENTS** This is a pleasant though uninspiring whiskey. This has obviously been designed to attract a maximum number of

agreeing to supply a very light Cooley blend to the British company Cellars International. Has been available in Northern Ireland since 1995.
(See also Royal Irish).

ERIN'S ISLE

At a time when Cooley was at its most vulnerable - the Government had decreed that a takeover by Irish Distillers would not have been in the country's best interests as far as monopolies were concerned - they needed some partners to come in with deals to raise much needed cash. The Scottish Distillers, Invergordon, had a sound background of providing blended whisky for supermarkets at the value-for-money end of the range and saw Cooley as an opening into the Irish section of the market. Starting in early 1995, they began investing in many barrels of Cooley whiskey and their blends are sculpted in Edinburgh by

respected blender Norman Mathieson assisted and abetted by Cooley blender Noel Sweeney. Norman admits that he blends his Irish as he would a Scotch, but when the ingredients are simply grain and pure malt, without any addition of traditional Irish pot still - that mercurial mixture of malted and unmalted barley - that is probably the safest and most sensible course to take.

TASTING NOTES ERIN'S ISLE

NOSE The light corn-grain is all consuming here. It is fresh and young with little or no pretension tomaturity. A trace of simple, pleasant malt.

TASTE Again the grain is quick off the starting blocks, leaving the malt trailing. After a shudderingly hard initial impact, it sweetens and the corn character becomes attractive and lush. The malt follows on hesitantly but vanishes quickly.

FINISH An austere, vodka-esque finish with the grain again having all the say. Some simple vanilla arrives as the palate dries.

COMMENTS This is a straight up and down whiskey. It is pleasant, though dependent on the high quality grain to make its mark. One from the Invergordon/Cooley family which depends on richness of the grain to add the necessary weight.

GOLDEN IRISH

Until the very last minute, this was going to hit the streets as "Old Irish", complete with label designed to that effect and showing a different character to the whiskey now found in bottle. Following the demise of Avoca, leading Irish store Dunne's were keen to land a popular Irish whiskey. The eventual style was ready in Dunne's stores shortly before Christmas 1996.

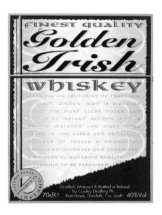

TASTING NOTES GOLDEN IRISH

NOSE Unquestionably of the Cooley ilk, similar to O'Briens but there is just the merest whiff of smoke on the malt. Rather attractive, dapper and well balanced.

TASTE The malt is as keen to show as the grain, though it is the grain which takes a dryish command towards the middle.

FINISH More grain and vanilla but with just a touch of malt and toffee lingering about.

COMMENTS The nose and the start of this whiskey offer much promise. But in reality it is let down a little by the grain being just a tad too forceful in the vital middle and finish. Despite this, a whiskey blend with a number of good points and certainly enjoyable. The weight, for its style, is just about right.

GREEN SPOT

Green Spot is to the true Irish whiskey drinker what an Irish Round Tower is to the archaeologist. It is a beautifully preserved, almost living, throwback to the old Ireland which takes some searching to locate, but once found, is an experience to savour. When I first discovered it in a shop in Galway, it was like finding all at once the pot of gold at the end of the rainbow.

Once upon a time in Ireland, many hundreds of wine merchants would fill their own casks with the spirit from their local distilleries and sell it under their own name, occasionally giving mention to the stills where it first bubbled into life. But all that changed when distillers became proprietorial and wished, often with good reason, due to the dubious practices of some merchants, to have complete control over any whiskey which bore their name. As businesses closed or merged, brands were lost. Others decided not to compete with the ever more powerful distillers. Sometimes distillers simply refused to supply the whiskey.

In the end, there was only one left which can still be found today. That sole survivor is Green Spot. There are no exact records as to when the brand first hit the streets, but certainly by the early 1920s the long-established wine merchants of Mitchell & Son of Kildare Street, Dublin, were annually putting to one side 100 sherry hogsheads to be filled at Jameson's Bow Street distillery. So the whiskey was not too overpowered by the wine, half of the casks used had held oloroso and other dark sherries, the other half were the former homes of lighter finos. The Jameson pot still whiskey would mature for five years in those casks before being vatted together and then allowed to blend and mature for a further five years in those same butts in Mitchell's old bonded warehouses in Fitzwilliam Lane.

The brand was initially known as Pat Whiskey, with a man looking very much the worse for wear apparently bursting through the label. Behind him was dark green shading. From this image grew the name Green Spot. The popularity of this type of whiskey spread to a seven-year-old Blue Spot, a Yellow Spot (12) and Red Spot (15).

As the costs involved in maturing expensive sherry casks became heavier and heavier, Mitchell reverted to vatting just the single and the original Green version. However, when Jameson switched production from Bow Street to Johns Lane the make-up of the whisky altered for the first time in living memory. Mitchell's maturing stocks were running low and, having no intention of losing their famous brand, the company entered into an agreement with Irish Distillers to produce the whiskey. A stipulation

TASTING NOTES GREEN SPOT

NOSE The first thing to strike you is the density of the nose: nothing light and flowery here. The pot still appears older than its eight years thanks to a pleasant dustiness (something similar to old Redbreast), and the influence of the sherry. All this is mixed with a curious menthol sub-stratum. Some evidence of bourbon wood around, too, but rather over-shadowed by this highly unusual cough-sweet malty effect.

TASTE Sweet, rich and full-bodied from the very start. It quickly fills the mouth with a glorious spiciness. All the time it somehow remains soft, though the tastebuds are constantly tweaked by a harder pot still maltiness. Wonderfully complex and busy.

FINISH Very long, dry and malty to start then sweetens and some late spice adds to all the fun. The very last, dying rays are rather cool on the throat, as if the menthol on the nose has returned.

COMMENTS This is a tremendous whiskey, sometimes even giving a sweet-honey feel more associated with Perthshire malts from Scotland. But the pot still is confident enough to confirm this as Irish with a maturity greater than the age of the whiskey used. If you see it, grab it. It's too much of a high-class one-off to ignore.

was that the whiskey supplied had to be matured in Midleton's own casks, but IDG were able to guarantee the future of the brand as pure single pot still whiskey.

The current Green Spot is made entirely from seven and eight-year-old Midleton pot still, a healthy 25 per cent coming from sherry cask, which is quite evident in its aroma and taste. With Irish Distillers producing their own 12-year-old pot still, Redbreast, it was understandable they were not willing to produce an older vatting for Mitchell's. But when Redbreast was taken off the market, Green Spot enjoyed the distinction of being the only, and very last, pure Irish Pot Still in existence. Now with Midleton back on the shelves it can no longer claim that, but it does remain the longest running pot still whiskey to continuously remain on the shelves.

Only 500 cases are made up each year, all for the home market with Galway, Limerick, Cork and Dublin being its main outposts. Those meagre 6,000 bottles represent a very small part of the Mitchell operation. But for a seventh-generation family company which dates back to 1805, it is one they cherish as a vital part of their own history and Ireland's whiskey heritage.

HEWITTS

The diversity of whiskeys produced within the Midleton Distillery is quite stunning. And with Hewitts, a whiskey of hitherto unsung beauty, we have another one-off. It is a heavier whiskey than many Irish blends and that is because this is a blend of two single malts and a single grain; the only whiskey IDG market from Midleton where there is no pot still whatsoever.

To achieve a balance, it is a blend of two types of malt: one light, the other heavy. The weight of the malt produced at Midleton is often determined by which part of the run off from the still, called the cut, is selected. To produce a lighter malt you narrow the cut from the very heart of the run. The more feints and foreshots you use, the heavier and oilier the spirit, and so the whiskey, becomes. The overall heaviness is further compounded by the amount of feints and

foreshots from the previous distillation put through the still. Whatever the case here, the vatted malt which goes into Hewitts from Midleton is heavier and more full-bodied than the malt from Bushmills which is also used in this brand. It is also deceptive in that the whiskeys used seem a lot more mature than the 6 to 10-year-olds actually used.

Hewitts was launched in the early 1960s purely for the home market. It was designed to do battle against Scotch and, originally, peated malt was used, though no more. Today it continues to be found only in Eire, where Munster is its heartland.

It was named after a gentleman called Thomas Hewitt, a merchant of Cork who, with two other entre-preneurial businessmen, founded the Watercourse Distillery in 1782. By 1868 the distillery was owned by the Hewitt family before it amalgamated that year with the city's three other distillers, North Mall, The Green and Daly's of John Street as well as the Midleton Distillery to form the Cork Distilleries Co.

Although Watercourse Distillery handed over the distilling reins to North Mall, it continued as a maltings and warehouse centre. In 1916 it began

TASTING NOTES HEWITTS

NOSE I love it: not only plenty of malt, but the heavy, plumy fruitiness and the clarity of it nestles perfectly with a grain whiskey which knows when to keep its distance whilst giving a distinct Irishness. Top rate stuff, this.

TASTE This is a blend which moulds itself around your mouth. You cannot escape from a single part of its extraordinary complexity and depth. It begins with a powerful malt theme, switching to sweet honey-fruit and then a peppery spiciness. None of this is laid back: it is all very forceful and confident.

FINISH The finish dries quite dramatically by comparison to the previous sweetness. The grain comes through with a particularly woody feel and is a comparative let-down to the all-round charisma of what has gone on before. Having said that, it's a long finish with some bourbony notes added in for good measure and it is never dull.

COMMENTS If you ever see this on the shelf of a bar or store, get it. It is totally unlike any other whiskey I have ever tasted in Ireland and certainly one of the most complex. It is in some ways the least Irish of any produced by IDG: even Bushmills and its associated blends show a pot still character for some unknown reason. This doesn't and I must say on the evidence of this, I wish Irish Distillers would bottle a single malt from Midleton now that Cooley has stolen Bushmills's thunder. Wonderful.

distilling again, only this time the output was grain whiskey. The remains of the distillery, including its chimney, can still be clearly seen along with most of the proud Victorian buildings, (some with the faded distillery lettering on them still). They have since been turned into a small industrial estate. But sadly its days are numbered: the remnants are due to be torn down in the near future to make way for a road.

INISHOWEN

For 70 years this old brand was little more than a footnote of Irish whiskey history. Once bottles from the famous old distiller Andrew A Watt could be found bearing this name. But in 1925 the old Irish company United Distilleries (no relation to today's multi-national company United Distillers) scrapped the brand. Shortly before Christmas 1995 it found its way back on the shelves, this time in the form of blended Irish whiskey and from Cooley. It was Watt who owned the Tyrconnell name and owned a racehorse by that name. Also in his stables could be found another thoroughbred - called Inishowen! This is a highly unusual blend by Irish standards: 20 per cent of the malt used in its make-up is peated.

There is something deliciously right about the name of the blend and its style and composition. The area of Inishowen, the most northerly part of Ireland, has for centuries been renowned for its much-prized poteen. So Cooley's unique addition of a smoky-peaty character fits in well there. And it would have been failing in its duty to history had it not been a blend of malt and grain whiskeys. In 1885 there was a legal battle over the Innishowen (with two *n*s) name when the Watt company sued an Irish spirits merchant. Watts whiskey was called "Watt's Old Innishowen" and the merchant's "O'Hanlon's Old Innishowen Malt." What was curious was that, in that period of time when adulteration was commonplace, the Watt's Old Inishowen was made entirely from

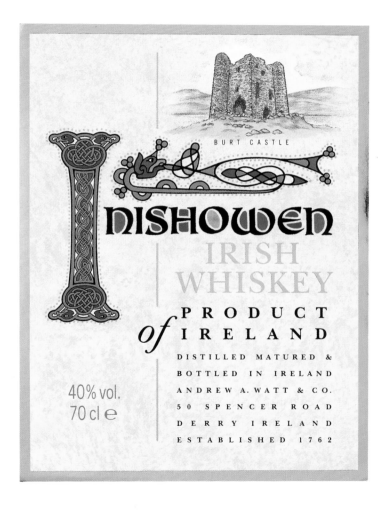

BURT CASTLE

INISHOWEN

IRISH
WHISKEY

PRODUCT
of IRELAND

DISTILLED MATURED &
BOTTLED IN IRELAND
ANDREW A. WATT & CO.
50 SPENCER ROAD
DERRY IRELAND
ESTABLISHED 1762

40% vol.
70 cl ℮

TASTING NOTES INISHOWEN

NOSE Unmistakable earthy yet lofty signs of peat are the first to show with grape and apple fruitiness not far behind. Simple traces of vanilla are also present.

TASTE Momentarily sweet then a dry, full, smoky, smouldering start with the malt also coming through. The grain has also gathered forces in the powerful middle.

FINISH Grainy, hard and uncompromisingly dry. The peat has retreated to just a spicy sparkle at the back of the tongue and a faint deep note with a touch of malty sweetness on the very end.

COMMENTS This is a real box of tricks, the only blended Irish where peat openly flaunts itself. The depth of peat has altered little on the palate since its launch, though the nose of the earlier bottlings was considerably more smoky. Genuinely lovely stuff for those with a favourable disposition towards heavier whiskeys, something not normally associated with Irish.

cheaper grain whiskey. The present mixture of both is now available in the usual Cooley-friendly countries of Ireland, Netherlands and Sweden as well as Iceland and even the United Arab Emirates.

JAMESON DISTILLERY

Just as the genesis of Irish whiskey cannot be told, lost as it is in uncharted history, it seems quite fitting that the very earliest days of the most famous name in Irish whiskey can be viewed with an equal lack of clarity. Read a different book, you will be told a different story. Whether Bow Street Distillery was founded by John Jameson or whether he took it over from others, is not at all important. What is important is the way the company became, by mid-Victorian times, not only one of the most

Left
The Jameson horse-drawn carriage is a familiar sight around Dublin.

dominant distillers in Ireland, but makers of one of the most consistently high-quality pot still spirits in the land.

When Alfred Barnard paid his visit in 1884 he was told the distillery was founded by three wealthy men including a Baronet and a General, and it was from them that the grandfather of the proprietors bought the business at the beginning

119

of the 19th century. However, a book partly produced by Jameson five years earlier dismissed that tale as no more than a "tradition" and admitted: "There is no one living who knows, and there is no discoverable documentary evidence to show, what was the date of foundation, neither can we even say at what date, prior to 1802, the distillery passed into the hands of the ancestor of the present proprietors."

However, it appears some evidence was discovered by the company which in 1924 published a detailed history and a shorter one some 26 years later, though both offered slightly differing accounts of Jameson's earliest days. It seems that the original John Jameson was a Scotsman from Alloa who had married into the Haig distilling dynasty and who, while still in his

30s, rose to the post of Sheriff Clerk of Clackmannanshire.

A confident man, he sought his fortune in Ireland, arriving in Dublin some time in the 1770s. His two sons, John and William, got to know a distiller by the name of John Stein operating in Bow Street and John, the elder of the two, married Stein's daughter Isabella. John Jameson senior took over the Bow Street Distillery around 1780 and was later succeeded by his son John. Brother William meanwhile ran a second Stein distillery at Marrowbone Lane which was to later bear his name after he gained control. Between them John and William Jameson forged the biggest distilling family in Irish history, though the Bow Street and Marrowbone Lane Distilleries were nothing less than business rivals.

There remain big question marks regarding the dates and order of things, although for over 50 years John Jameson & Son has settled upon 1780 as the year of the company's formation.

Certainly by 1810 John Jameson was operating a 1,256-gallon still making pot still whiskey, and when in production 11 years later, it was the second largest in all Ireland. Strangely, the biggest of all was operated by Jameson and Dewar, doubtless another but less well-known branch of the family.

The distillery continued to prosper and was in perfect financial health, enabling expansion in the latter half of the 19th century as the popularity of Irish whiskey grew worldwide. By the mid-1880s

Opposite

The old Bow Street Distillery which grew to gargantuan proportions during its 200-year history. The red building in the middle now houses the Jameson Heritage Centre.

the distillery had become quite enormous. It took 300 people to run it and some one million gallons of spirit were produced each year. The whiskey was double-distilled in a still room boasting four enormous stills: the wash stills held 24,000 gallons each with the low wines stills 14,500 and 13,000 gallons respectively. Because the stills were so large, not only were they heated directly by coal fires from below, but they also used internal steam coils, a practice which was way ahead of its time.

Throughout all this expansion and expense, Jameson and Son had remained very much a family concern. But at last it became a private limited company in 1891 and a public company 11 years later. During this time the size of the distillery grew and grew and its remains, of castle-like proportions, can still be found between Bow Street and Smithfield, its entrances now bricked up, where once the massive arches fronted narrow cobbled streets and lanes.

Opposite
Jameson hits the
mark – a 1930s
showcard.

The cellars which ran warren-like below Dublin's streets were long famed for their holding of Jameson's prized whiskeys. The company had been slow to bottle under their own name preferring to sell their make to merchants who bottled it themselves under a wide variety of titles. But even so, never did its reputation ever diminish. Along with Power's, it was considered the finest Irish pot still whiskey money could buy. But in 1966 came the famous merger and five years later the extraordinarily long tradition of whiskey production at Bow Street Distillery,

spanning perhaps some 200 years, came to an end. For a while Jameson whiskey was produced just across the Liffey by Power's until that, too, closed and Midleton in Ireland's deep south became its new and unlikely home.

When Barnard began his tour of Ireland his first stop was Bow Street. But it is a strange fact that before he arrived he made the small detour to St Michan's Church where, in the legendary crypt, he

Why be
an oddity?

most people
prefer Jameson

Above
The famous
Jameson slogan
illustrated by
Rex Whistler.

gazed upon the mummified remains of several bodies including a nun and a crusader, with their features, skin and nails, still intact. Just yards away stood the busiest distillery in the world, a picture of Victorian vitality, hope and grandeur.

When I retraced Barnard's steps in researching this book I touched the same leathered hands when I found those mummies in an almost identical state of suspended decay as he had. Outside it was a quite different matter, however. The distillery buildings, bar those now turned into offices and a museum, were barely intact and had suffered horribly since the distillery's closure only 20 years ago. Their magnificent, classic proportions are still there to admire, but for how much longer?

Yet while the mummies remain entombed, silent and soulless, at least the spirit of Jameson lives on, albeit 125 miles away.

JAMESON

It is hard to believe that the world's top selling Irish whiskey was not introduced onto the market in bottled form until as recently as 1968. For centuries Jameson sold their whiskey by the cask and individual bonding companies then sold Jameson under their own labels around the world.

The Jameson company did hit back by initially introducing Crested Ten, but it was the introduction of Red Seal, in a design similar to the present Jameson bottling, which lit the touch paper for success.

Although Jameson always came second to Power's in popularity in the home Irish market, it achieved much greater acclaim abroad. So when Pernod-Ricard took over Irish Distillers in 1988, they made the commercial decision to plough all their marketing resources behind two whiskeys: Jameson and Bushmills.

TASTING NOTES JAMESON

NOSE A really delightful layer of very clean, very fresh sherry has given this some extra weight and quality. Dig deeper and a strata of pot still is evident as is, eventually, the grain which is likewise clean and crisp. Intriguing hints of honeyed marzipan help give the softest of fruitcake characters.

TASTE Deliciously mouth-filling and mouthwatering from the start with the pot still playing a far greater role than the nose suggests. The sweetness is superbly balanced and a constant and only as the whiskey pans out does some extra, drier sherry traces begin to make their mark. Quite substantial and bordering on, perhaps even reaching, being a complex whiskey.

FINISH This is where the grain starts to be noticed. But there is nothing harsh here and the sherry and barley notes extend the length of the finale. However, the sherry does ensure that nothing too off-key or unforgiving gets through.

The result is that Jameson accounts for nearly 75 per cent of all Irish whiskey sold. Apart from its high marketing profile, its success can also be put down to some judicious blending: it has been specifically designed to appeal to as wide a cross-section of people as possible. Its pot still/grain content is about 50/50, although a trademark softness suggests the grain has the greater say and a large number of fresh ex-bourbon casks are used which would help dampen down some of the pot still's higher notes. For years I had been told that even some malt from Bushmills went into this blend but I have recently been corrected that this has never been the case. Sherry-casked whiskey is used here as well, to around the 10 per cent mark.

COMMENTS Over the years I have criticised Jameson. Sometimes in the past I have felt it too bland, designed not to offend too many people. Sometimes (especially during 1995) I was pleasantly surprised by the amount of invigorating pot still I could pick out, though ultimately disappointed by the unwieldy nature of the grain. There has, however, been a change in Jameson. An almost microscopic one which may not be recognised at first. But it is there. For some years Irish Distillers have followed a policy of maturing some of their stocks in new ultra-fresh Oloroso casks. That investment is beginning to show. Usually, I prefer to leave sherry out of whiskeys and let the natural character of the grain have its say. A little pot still has been lost on the nose and the finish, which is regrettable. These may have been sacrificed for the overall good of the whiskey: there is a complexity now in Jameson where before there had been none. The pot still abounds impressively at the very first and the way the sherry muscles in is lovely. Maybe the finish could be a little fuller and pot still rich. A very drinkable whiskey with a new-found degree of elegance.

JAMESON CRESTED TEN

The Irish are a lucky people. I can count the number of times I've seen this whiskey in pubs in England, Scotland and Wales on both hands. In Ireland, though, and the Republic in particular, it is in a great many pubs and bars and is regarded as something a little bit special – which it certainly is. Sadly, it appears to be only older men – 40s and

upwards – who drink it. This is odd when you consider that this has an all-round appeal to suit anyone who enjoys a rich pot still character with some confident sherry. There is even a slight sweetness which just might appeal to women.

Perhaps it's a matter of perception: Crested Ten is Jameson's oldest bottled brand in Ireland. It was launched in 1963 to meet Power's Gold Label and Paddy head on and it was that generation which first learned about its delightful charms. Although other drinkers have followed suit, it is the standard Jameson brand which has taken seniority status by way of sales.

Crested Ten is more expensive than standard Jameson. The whiskeys used in it begin at 8 years old and the above average sherry-cask pot still is aged anything between 10 and 15 years. Also there is more pot still than grain. This is a whiskey which traditionally sells well in the winter but is sufficiently light in character and generally too good to be ignored in the summer.

AN A-Z OF DISTILLERIES & BRANDS

TASTING NOTES JAMESON CRESTED TEN

NOSE An impressive sherry start is well matched by pot still sharpness, spice and a hint of melon and ginger. Deliciously Irish.

TASTE Sits in the mouth wonderfully, kicking off with an extremely soft sherry-maltiness and then becomes quite warm and spicy. Throughout there is a delightful sweetness which is perfectly counter-balanced by a rumbling buzz of spice and some brooding bourbon-chocolate notes.

FINISH Extremely classy. The grain does start making an impact here but this is high quality stuff and seemingly well aged and mild-mannered. The sherry also decides to come back for a short encore.

COMMENTS A whiskey of great finesse which is balanced beautifully between sweet and dry, light notes and heavy ones. Like all great Irish whiskeys, for the most satisfying results, this should not be sipped but taken by the mouthful and swallowed slowly.

JAMESON 1780

In the mid 1980s Jameson had a problem. For years they had been selling a 12-year-old which had been distilled at their old Bow Street Distillery. It was quite a heavy whiskey with some sherry character. But Bow Street had been closed for some time and stocks were becoming dangerously low. A replacement whiskey was required. Jameson also produced an even heavier 15-year-old and it would not be long before it was impossible to keep that going as well. So the company decided to scrap both whiskeys and produce a 12-year-old which would stand out as their premier brand.

Today Jameson 1780 remains just that. It has a pot still/sherry infusion like no other whiskey on earth and of all their current blends has the closest

TASTING NOTES JAMESON 1780

NOSE Lush and confident, spicy and warming, there is a prevailing oloroso undercurrent from which it is hard to pull away.

TASTE A whiskey which fills the mouth first with sweet sherry, then the unmistakable delights of old pot still coupled with a short but effective flypast of spice. The pot still dominates, quite a trick when the sherry is so evident. Full-bodied and hard to spot the grain.

FINISH Medium length to long; yet the pot still hangs around, but as it loosens its grip first the sherry comes back on song; then that too fades and the grain makes a dry, vanilla-intense contribution.

COMMENTS It is all too easy to overdo the sherry but this is a whiskey of great charm and poise which has got everything in proportion. I rate Irish Distiller's blender Barry Walsh one of the best in the world. When he told me he regards this whiskey as his favourite, I was not surprised. Much hard work and skill has gone into getting this one right. Excellent.

characteristics to the old Bow Street distillate. At least a third of the casks used in this brand are ex-sherry and pot still whiskey accounts for 75 per cent of the blend. Boasting an age statement of 12 years, the average age of the whiskeys used is way above that, with healthy amounts of the older whiskeys included, some of them going as far back as 1976 distillations. This started life as a whiskey designed for the Irish market and today is found all too rarely abroad, although I have spotted it in some duty free stores.

Jameson Distillery Reserve

It is not often you will see this whiskey on someone's sideboard or in a bar. This is probably the most exclusive of all Irish whiskies. Created in 1992 to mark the opening of the Jameson Heritage Centre at Midleton Distillery, the style is very close to the Jameson 1780, though for my money it is not so well balanced.

But if anyone is a great fan of heavily sherried whiskey, then this is the ultimate experience as far as Ireland is concerned. The make-up is similar to 1780 with over a third of all the whiskey used having been matured in ex-sherry casks and around 75 per cent of the blend being pot still. My guess is that the sherry casks are the fullest bodied oloroso they can find, hence the sweetness and intensity. Certainly the pot still plays a less important role than the 1780.

As it can be bought only at the distillery, sales are relatively low and this helps explain why such sherry-rich casks have been selected. They don't have to vat this one very often so they can be more selective. A must for any serious whiskey drinker.

TASTING NOTES DISTILLERY RESERVE

NOSE Another intense sherry start with the sweet wine being a little more heavy-handed than the 1780. Despite the sherry dominance, the Irish pot still comes through loud and clear. A little grain also makes its presence felt, as do delicious and warming peppers.

TASTE It begins honey-sweet and rich, though not overly complex. Apart from the sherry and pot still, few other notes come through at first, but this is a brooding whiskey, heavy and intense.

FINISH Some grain returns but there is an unusual saltiness about. It dries quite dramatically and where many Irish whiskeys are let down by their finish this certainly isn't. It is the most complex part of the malt, refusing to die with sweet and sour waves lapping against the tastebuds until the tide, after what seems an age, decides to go out. Wonderful stuff.

COMMENTS This is the Macallan of the Irish whiskey world. Easily the most sherry-dominant of all the country's whiskeys. Oddly the middle, although no slouch, is the most disappointing, but the finish is something else.

JAMESON 12-YEAR-OLD

A sister company of Irish Distillers in the Pernod-Ricard stable is World Brands Duty Free. When they specified a new whiskey for the Far Eastern market, based on the established Jameson 1780 with a bit more "oomph", that's just what they got. Unveiled in 1996, this is made heavier not just by the type and amount of sherry used, but the introduction of some weighty Jameson pot still.

TASTING NOTES

NOSE A delightful intermingling of rich pot still tones and subtle sherry. For a whiskey of this age, the oak plays only a limited role, though can be detected with a gentle sweetening vanilla and spices among the sturdier grain and heavier fruit. The aroma does show more wine as it warms in the hand. But it is the pot still which continues to dominate. Magnificent.

TASTE Massive stuff, sheer dynamite. The fireworks that explode around the palate are again pot still-based, though the grain comes through with a hint of coffee. There is the faintest hint of honey too. The unmalted barley does create the backbone by which all else hangs. And there is a lot of meat: with the fruity middle being helped along by the very subtle sherry presence. Succulent and melt-in-the-mouth.

FINISH A long finish that carries on the same theme with the pot still keeping charge. Those coffee tones in the middle become cocoa ones at the finish. Some bitter oak and unmalted barley end things with a flourish.

COMMENTS The new range of Jameson whiskeys do not stint on complexity. Against the sweeter and more sherry-dominant 12-year-old Distillery Reserve and the trusty, wonderful old Jameson 1780, also a 12-year-old, this is ground-breaking stuff. The others are genuinely great whiskeys, but relative plodders on the tastebuds compared to the array of mouth-watering charac-teristics to be savoured with this latest creation.

JAMESON GOLD

This whiskey was originally designed to wow the Asians in the Far East duty free shops and in developmental stage was known as Jameson XO. Under a far more appropriate name it can be found in duty free outlets closer to Irish shores, having been launched during 1996. This was a stage two from the earlier Jameson Marconi and consists of whiskies ranging from 10 to 13 years old. Although there is significant amount of sherry cask used, it is the 10-year-old virgin American oak casks first sparingly used in Marconi which sets this whiskey apart from any other on the market. There has been confident use of Irish pot still to ensure a very delicate and crisp character. Because there is so little of this new wood in stock, Jameson Gold can never be produced in amounts to satisfy anything other than duty free. Which is a tragedy for us all.

TASTING NOTES JAMESON GOLD

NOSE In a word, stunning! There is a rich, full pot still character one normally prays for in a Jameson and it arrives healthily and kept in good company by ripe, juicy sultanas, a yeasty fruitiness and a dollop of acacia honey.

TASTE Sweet, crisp start with the unmalted barley arriving first. Then there is an eruption in the mouth as a massive wave of rich creamy oils and honey take over the proceedings. The malt hangs gallantly onto the middle but is overwhelmed by the richness of honey and berry fruit and hints of clementines. The mouthfeel is different to any other whiskey currently on the market. None have such a fingerprint in being at once crisp and oily. This is truly unique stuff.

FINISH Very long with the firmness and vague bitterness of the unmalted barley being the one constant throughout from start to finish. There is even a peppery finale to round things off.

COMMENT For years Power's was my number one Irish blend. It has now been ruthlessly shoved into second place by a whiskey which must rank in the top 10 of the world's whiskeys, the top five of the world's blends. No words I put here can do justice to its complexity. This whiskey has a touch of everything, in just about perfect proportions. I have said blender Barry Walsh is one of the world's finest blenders. This, his latest creation, proves the point. An absolute masterpiece.

TASTING NOTES JAMESON MARCONI

NOSE This is how I love a blended Irish nose: lashings of pot still but fattened out by lush, grainy notes. There is also a touch of sherry to add both fruit and weight plus warming peppers. The cleanness is something like the aroma you get from the flour created at the mill. Entirely different to any other whiskey bearing the Jameson crest.

TASTE Ethereally light start with the grain getting some early vanilla into play. But the pot still is quite boisterous and doesn't hang around in adding a cutting edge to the palate. When warmed in the hand and allowed to breathe for a time in the glass gentler, sweeter, honey notes become apparent.

JAMESON MARCONI

It is a little known fact that Guglielmo Marconi had an ever greater claim to fame than being the inventor of radio. He was also the great grandson of John Jameson. On his mother's side, of course. His world-changing discovery was made in 1895 and the bottle marks the 100th anniversary of this feat. The broadcast from Ireland to Nova Scotia, smartly depicted in gold on the green bottle came a little later, I believe. The whiskey has seen active service only in duty free and from a very small vatting little now remains. This should not be confused with other embossed Jameson bottles to be found in duty free; those are also limited edition embossed bottles called the Jameson Distillery Collection and contain standard Jameson whiskey. Marconi, however, is anything but standard. Blender Barry Walsh used it as the

FINISH It is in the finish that things begin to really happen. There is an unmistakable juicy barley character, almost chewy, and the older grain adds a deft touch of chocolate. It is the pot still, as ever, in this style of whiskey, which hangs around to plant the flag. Gripping stuff.

COMMENTS Although this was an early stopping off point in the championship race to achieve Jameson Gold, ultimately there is a vast difference between the two whiskeys. As tasty and mouthwatering as this whiskey is, it is only the interesting outline of the honey that sets Gold apart from its fellow spirit. Nor does it hang together quite so effortlessly. Usually I prefer whiskies to be slightly warmed in the hand. This brings out their fullest, richest character.

This whiskey works best, though, when drunk cool, without ice. Then the grain and pot still gang together to really give the tastebuds a metallic charge. It is invigorating stuff.

cast on which to finally mould the magnificent Jameson Gold. There is no mistaking the family link, especially the liberal use of very sharp, full-flavoured pot still. Fittingly, to mark the anniversary of an innovator a new type of Irish whiskey was used for the very first time: pot still whiskey matured in virgin American oak.

JONES ROAD DISTILLERY

When, on July 22, 1873 the newly-formed Dublin Whiskey Distillery Company began their first ever mash, it was quite a remarkable achievement because it was exactly one year to the day prior to this that the building of Dublin's last, and in many ways grandest, distilleries had begun.

While nearly all of Dublin's other major whiskey distilleries had been started as family concerns, Jones Road was different. It had been built purely as a commercial venture by a group of Dublin businessmen, including a couple of accountants, with no distilling knowledge who employed skilled whiskey men.

The location of the distillery was by far the most breathtaking, and historic, in the city. The site, surrounded by the ruins of a castle and abbey, was on the very spot of the Battle of Clontarf, where in 1014, Danish invaders were dealt a mortal blow by King Brian Boru.

To add to the beautiful views from the distillery, (it was even compared by contemporary writers to the Bay of Naples!), the River Tolka flowed through its grounds, although the water for making the whiskey was piped in from the Royal Canal a mile away, thus sharing its water source with John Jameson.

However, as trading became tougher, drastic action was needed at the new distillery. The merger of Power's and Jameson in 1966 was not the first time Dublin distilling giants had forged a partnership. In 1889 DWD merged with two long distillers in the city, William Jameson and George Rowe, to form the Dublin Distilling Company. But they continued to produce pure pot still under their own names.

Although between them they had the capacity to produce 3,500,000 gallons each year, lack of demand meant they achieved nowhere near that figure. The company limped through the early 20th century, closing one, then another, of the distilleries, sometimes reopening them to produce small quantities of new spirit. The company was wound up near the end of the Second World War.

Distilled in 1942 and bottled in 1991 this 65 per cent abv whiskey is available from William Cadenhead. It is also sold in miniature bottles. However, when it comes to whiskey, age does not always come before beauty and this is a 48-year-old Irish that should be kept in the bottle as a keepsake for the historical significance of its contents. It has spent just too long in the cask to be drinkable.

KELLY'S

An Invergordon brand with whiskey, as ever, from Cooley's warehouses. This is marketed exclusively by the Dutch cash-and-carry chain, Makro, and can be found throughout Europe following its launch during 1996. The format is very similar to the supermarket whiskeys supplied by Cooley and Invergordon.

TASTING NOTES KELLY'S

NOSE There is no stinting in the grain character of this blend. The malt, however, does become involved sufficiently to add a grassy sweetness to the proceedings. Good balance.

TASTE Light and ethereal even on the tastebuds. Everything lands and takes off with all the delicacy of a butterfly. There is hardly anything offering weight or substance but this is refreshing and attractive nonetheless.

FINISH Short to medium with lots of evidence of ex-bourbon cask being extensively used thanks to a late cocoa character.

COMMENTS What can you say? Another Cooley-Invergordon brand with all the family traits. It does enjoy an element of good quality and, above all, balance. Even so, it remains best to be slugged as a refreshing restorative or something to keep you going before dinner is served.

KILBEGGAN DISTILLERY

It is impossible to visit John Locke's Kilbeggan distillery and fail to be moved. It is as if the making of Irish whiskey from a century or more ago has been held in a time-warp. Kilbeggan may be the Gaelic for "little church", but it is a cathedral among the world's distilleries. As it sits proud and splendid beside the River Brusna, it is a picture of charm and tranquillity, but once it was a place of intrigue and dubious practice. Although there was never a bad word said against the whiskey it made, those who ran it were much maligned and in the 1950s, when money was tight and the distillery needed all the help it could get, it fell by the wayside, tarnished by the many unproved accusations.

How a distillery is founded and builds up a great name is a fascinating tale often involving people of extraordinary insight and energy. Kilbeggan is no different, but as distilleries go, it is the events of its later years which catch the imagination.

It began life in 1757 as a more modest concern than the fine old building that can be seen today. It is thought the man behind it was Gustavus Lambert, the most important landowner in the immediate district. As the first distillery was built, materials from an old Cistercian monastery on the site were used to aid construction.

Above

An old Locke's advertisement making a poetic sales pitch rhyming "sure" with "pure". W B Yeats can rest soundly.

John Locke's involvement in the distillery dates from the mid 19th-century and it was he who built it into a business of major importance in the Irish whiskey trade. Its highs and lows, though, reflected the turbulence of the Irish whiskey market with the fortunes of the company peaking, like so many other distillers, between the 1860s and the turn of the century.

The 1920s and '30s were make or break years for Ireland's distillers. Most of them broke. Somehow Locke's clung on, even though their trading, like their management, was weak. They survived only by the strength of their good name, but there was limited demand for Irish pot still

whiskey and what demand there was appeared to be satisfied by Power's and Jameson. The end of the Second World War and Locke's fortunate situation as an operational company should have put them in a position to flourish since there was a worldwide shortage of whiskey. But the company found itself without sufficient stocks to capitalize on this rare opening. One reason, Andrew Bielenberg claims in his history of the distillery, was because much of the whiskey it produced was being siphoned off for the black market. The alleged scam was being worked by middle-management with the aid of the revenue officer. While they grew rich, the company was being bled dry.

Left
The resplendent Kilbeggan (Gaelic for "little church") Distillery by the banks of the Brusna was built with materials from an old monastery on the site.

If Bielenberg's claims are true the capping irony was that while it went on undetected for years, the name of the distillery finally fell into disrepute after being implicated in a scandal of which it was entirely innocent. In 1947 the distillery had at last been put up for sale as a going concern. The best offer came from a Swiss syndicate but what initially looked like a straightforward business transaction turned firstly into a farce, then a whodunnit and finally a matter of rancour and uproar within the Irish Government. When a £75,000 deposit was not forthcoming from the Swiss, the solicitor and auctioneer dealing with the sale began to smell a rat. They alerted both police and officials from the Department of Justice.

When the syndicate's interpreter was found, it was discovered he was travelling on a forged English passport. He had given his name as Horace Smith, but in fact he was Alexander Maximoe, wanted by the British police. On his deportation to Britain he managed to disappear on the Holyhead ferry and at first was thought dead. It transpired, however, that he had been picked up by another boat in which he had arranged to make his escape.

Since the auctioneer involved in the mystery was a Fianna Fail senator, his political enemies tried to make capital out of the strange goings on. A tribunal was set up to look into why the Irish Government appeared happy to sell one of Ireland's most famous names to foreigners of questionable integrity. The findings were that the syndicate's sole aim was to sell the stocks of 60,000 gallons of whiskey on the British black market. Although the Government was cleared of any improper dealings the mud stuck and the Fianna Fail party, which was already having a rough time of it, lost even more support.

It was also the end of the road for the distillery. It limped on until 1953 when the stills were shut down for the last time. Some of the whiskey stocks were sold off, but some remained at the distillery

and this was finally sold with the buildings to a Karl Heinz Mellow for a mere £10,000 in 1963. He marketed this ageing pot still as Old Galleon, a few cases of which were sold in Ireland, the majority off-loaded in Germany.

Meanwhile the famous old distillery was turned, literally, into a pigsty. Porkers lived in the converted buildings for years. The distilling apparatus was left untouched until the early 70s when the four pot stills were sold to a scrap dealer. Just a week later the copper market failed. If only copper prices had dropped a week before, these marvellous artefacts might still be in existence.

By the 1980s the possibilities of turning the distillery into a museum – and bringing tourists into the Irish midlands – were plainly clear. The

Kilbeggan Development Association rented the distillery from its new owner Powerscreen and began renovations. In 1987 Cooley Distillery bought the entire site from the directors of Powerscreen and since then the old Kilbeggan Distillery has been part of the whiskey industry. Work began on changing the warehouses to accommodate Cooley's forthcoming distillate and by the early 1990s the deafening hammering of coopers repairing damaged casks could once again be heard reverberating around the ancient buildings. Meanwhile Cooley had agreed to lease other sections of the building, mainly those holding the old mash tun and fermenters, back to the KDA for a peppercorn rent of £1 a year for the next 99 years in order to preserve the distillery as a vital site of industrial archaeology.

The redundant old pot stills from Tullamore were brought by Cooley to Kilbeggan and it was hoped that one day distilling could begin again at John Locke's old distillery. Plans have been drawn up to make a traditional pot still whiskey at a cost of £1.5 million. There are now cheaper plans afoot to mash and ferment the pot still at Cooley and bring the wash to Kilbeggan to distil in the old Tullamore stills.

But with Cooley having problems enough keeping their own plant operational it seems very unlikely. But wouldn't life be a dull thing without the occasional romantic dreams of the optimist and visionary? After all, wasn't that how most distilleries began in Ireland?

John Locke's and Kilbeggan

The future is always more important than the past as far as spirit brands are concerned and there are no more vital examples of this in Irish whiskey than Locke's and Kilbeggan. Once, they were two famous names slugging it out in a shrinking market. Today, after a long period of obsolescence, they are exactly the opposite and represent an extraordinary breakthrough in the ending of the monopolistic control of Irish whiskey. Tyrconnell single malt was the first out of the Cooley stable only because they had to wait a while longer for their oldest grain stocks to mature to the three years minimum required by law.

The actual arrival of Kilbeggan and Locke's on the market was delayed by Irish Distillers' unsuccessful attempt to buy out Cooley Distillery and smother the brands at birth. Monopoly regulations have for the meantime prevented IDG's moves, but Cooley must now perform in overseas markets in a way that IDG have so far failed to do if they are to remain independent and a cash influx must be forthcoming if Cooley is to survive. Aside from these considerations things have started well. Over the next year Kilbeggan will be found in the Netherlands, Switzerland, Northern Ireland, USA, France, Germany and in the UK Locke's should soon be making an entry.

Older Irish drinkers will remember both these brands as pure pot still. They are now both blends with Locke's being a slightly heavier version of

Kilbeggan. The brands were sculpted by independent blender Jimmy Lang, once of Chivas and creator of the famous Passport Scotch brand, with the aid of Noel Sweeney of Cooley Distillery. For these blends Jimmy used some of the slightly later malts which had improved greatly from the first run. Considering he had only a single malt and single grain to work from, it was a pretty impressive first go. As the malt and grain matures the blends look set to get better and better, a fairly lip-smacking prospect.

TASTING NOTES

NOSE What a disappointing nose: astringent, flat and uninspiring. There is some malt in there, but really, it is pretty apologetic stuff.

TASTE Oily and malty to start with, a pleasing sweetness that fits well into the scheme of things. Toffee arrives by the cart-load to flatten everything out.

FINISH Medium length with lots of toffee, some impressive bourbony notes filter through.

COMMENTS This is not a patch on what it was. When first launched, complete with identical poor nose, it has absolutely enormous character that danced a jig on the tastebuds. Now its best feature is its bourbon traits towards the middle and finish.

TASTING NOTES

NOSE Traces of sweet oloroso plus some grassy malt overpowers the clean grain.

TASTE There is an excellent lushness to this where the malt moves freely around the palate, picking up some sweet honey notes on its journey. The grain comes into play a little later to form a brick-hard middle.

FINISH The dryness persists with some genuine oaky tones coming through. There is some cocoa bitterness that can be recognised in other Cooley blends, like Millar's, but it is in total harmony with the constant bitter-sweet theme that picks up from the middle.

COMMENTS There is no doubt this whiskey has changed shape two or three times since it was first devised. The very first version offered a rather mean finish to quite a malty blend.

Phase II saw a more complete Irish with enormous chocolate and vanilla character as the grain had easily the biggest part to play. This is Phase III, a sweeter whiskey which has achieved great balance as the malt once more has a far greater say. A highly delicious and dangerously more-ish whiskey which will remain in the taste-buds.

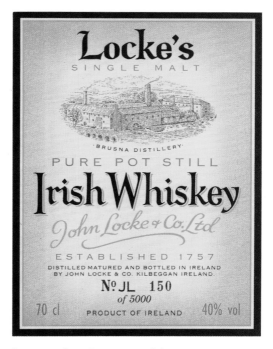

LOCKE'S SINGLE MALT LIMITED EDITION

This whiskey was launched by Cooley as a limited edition of 5,000 bottles to bring in some much needed cash fast. Something like eleven casks went into the making of this single malt, each hand-picked from the original fillings of the distillery's first year, 1989. Vatted as a 3-year-old in 1992, it is very hard to find, though Cooley do have a number remaining in stock. Each costs around the £50 mark.

TASTING NOTES
LOCKE'S SINGLE MALT LIMITED EDITION

NOSE: The kind of nose that bulges with character. It is enormously oily for a start. Some purists may say the distillate was not quite perfect. They would be right. Having said that, I love the big fruit-barley character; it is like a fruit loaf or hot cross bun.

TASTE That oiliness immediately clings to every edge of the mouth. The barley is big and succulent. There is a peculiar copper-tanginess, as well: as if the spirit has had massive contact with that particular metal.

FINISH The malt is nothing short of enormous with very little else coming through. However, there is a tang which is not quite right. Again it is metallic but also certain oils that you cannot help but feel should not be there.

COMMENTS If this was offered to me in a blind tasting among single malt Scotches I would never be able to tell the difference. It has a clear malt-intense, vaguely grassy Speyside style. My other guess would be that it came from new or very small stills, or both, because there is definitely the feel of copper in this. It is not unpleasant; you can spot it through the deepness of intensity. Very unusual. A very tasty dram. But one ultimately let down a little by the finish. At full stretch on the palate, though, it is quite delicious and the sheer intensity of the malt is sublime.

MIDLETON DISTILLERY

The town of Midleton, located as it is a mile or two inland from the south coast and equidistant between Cork and Youghal, hence its name, is one like any other you might find in Ireland. It has a main thoroughfare in which all the shops can be found and the pavements, as seems peculiar to Ireland, are constantly busy by day with people going about their everyday business, and by night the streets are crowded as the many pubs are visited and revisited.

The buildings are well constructed and pleasing to the eye, especially when the sun illuminates them, but are by no means outstanding. Tucked away, though, behind the shops on the east side of the main street lie not one, but two distilleries. The one that can be seen through the gates as you cross the old bridge which has taken you into Midleton from the Cork road has a splendour about it which momentarily halts you in your tracks. But on entering the building, you would fear that this is just another Kilbeggan: ancient, proud but obsolete.

Opposite
A bottle of whiskey bonded in 1922 from the original Midleton Distillery.

But whereas virtually every other town in Ireland has at one time or another, over the last 200 years, failed, Midleton somehow has succeeded. It still makes whiskey. But not in the 18th-century buildings which boast its original stills because a few hundred yards beyond some trees sits the distillery which now accounts for the spirit which matures to make up the whiskey for all the Jameson brands – Paddy, Power's, Midleton

Rare, Hewitts, Dunphys, Redbreast, Green Spot, and Tullamore Dew.

Unique to any distillery in the world, these stills are not only the last to make pure Irish pot still – a mixture of malted and unmalted barley – but when required they also produce a pure single malt and, in the patent stills, produce varying types of grain whiskey to suit individual blends.

Why Midleton should have survived is really a matter of good fortune and fate. It has always been known for making good pot still, but no better than some distilleries which were well known to drinkers four or five generations ago or long forgotten names now found as brands that are much lighter blends. To the purist, it must seem unjust and ironic that these distilleries, purpose-built by men of vision and often at great personal hardship, should today be lost or at best lie in varying states of rack and ruin, while Midleton may have never become a distillery at all had not Marcus Lynch's textile business failed. But let us be thankful it ever made whiskey at all.

IRISH WHISKY.

CORK DISTILLERIES CO. Ltd.
Midleton Distillery.

Date of Bonding ....

Bonded at ... 25.9.2 ?

HEAD OFFICE:
Morrison's Island, CORK.

It was Lynch who, for the then massive outlay of £20,000, erected the sturdy buildings of Midleton after leasing the site from Viscount Midleton on May 20, 1796. The woollen manufacturing business had been operating for only a short while before the British army, expanding its forces to meet the threat of Napoleon, bought the land and the mill which it converted into barracks for soldiers and stabling for their horses.

Lynch was later able to lease back the buildings but by the 1820s the mill was lying empty, free from both the captains of industry and of warfare. The Government sold the property to the Archbishop of Cashel and on his death his brother, Lord Midleton, was again able to acquire the land. He had not had it long before he sold it to three brothers, James, Daniel and Jeremiah Murphy on December 20, 1825. It was they who knew exactly the purpose the fine buildings should be turned to: the making of whiskey.

One of the most astonishing features of the distillery is a cast-iron water-wheel built in 1852 to replace the old wooden one. It was the Murphys who secured the use of the waterway needed to turn it, and in turn power the raking equipment inside the mash tuns.

When Daniel retired from the firm, the distillers called themselves James Murphy & Co. It was continued as a strictly family concern, although some members left the distilling side to set up the Murphy Brewery in Cork. But although they were a close-knit family, they were very astute business partners and it was James Murphy who hit upon consolidating the company by merging it with the distilleries operating in Cork.

The Cork distillers of North Mall, The Watercourse, The Green and Daly's, all saw the economic wisdom behind the move and the possibility of closing operating plants, shedding jobs and thus saving money. In those days distilling was labour intensive, employing between 150 and 300 people at every distillery. After a series of meetings they finalised their plans and on December 23, 1867, just days after Murphy's 42nd anniversary, the Cork Distilleries Company was formed, with Murphy's officially being sold into the group the following year.

James Murphy was appointed the CDC's first managing director and the company thrived. Distilling was confined to just the two plants, Midleton and North Mall which continued to make its then world-famous Wise's Cork Old Pot-Still Whisky (sic). Watercourse ceased distilling but carried on malting and warehousing, and the making of whiskey also stopped at both the Green Distillery and Daly's which were used for warehousing and as granaries.

That Midleton should have continued distilling is not really that surprising. Situated in the countryside it was not subject to city overheads and perhaps more importantly, the wash still holding 31,648 gallons was not only the largest pot still in Ireland, but also the whole world. The distillery with a Coffey still on site had access as

well to the making of blended whiskey if so
desired. For over 100 years nothing really changed
at Midleton. The Coffey still was replaced, as late
as 1962, by a German-made continuous still, but
that was the extent of the changes made. The
whiskey continued to be made in their giant wash

Left
The old cast iron water-wheel at Midleton Distillery was built in 1852, replacing the old wooden one, to power the racking equipment inside the mash tuns.

still and even the men responsible for its quality were all members of one family. In the 1880s it was a Mr A Ross, whose own father had managed Midleton, who escorted Alfred Barnard around the distillery and it was Sandy Ross, whose father had also been the manager, who was the site superintendent of the distillery nearly a century later as it entered its final days.

Ireland is well known for its tall tales and miracles. None, though, are more astonishing than the one regarding Sandy, who was fortunate in the extreme to still be around to follow in his father and grandfather's footsteps. He was working in the still room standing beside a pot still when the copper exploded and he was blown clean out of the building through a window. Just moments before, he had been going about his daily business, but seconds later found himself on the cold gravel outside, surrounded by a cluster of startled and amused work mates. Worse still, he was naked save for a shirt collar that gripped limpet-like to his neck and the belt of his trousers that hung limply around his waist. Apart from a few scratches and his bruised dignity, he was otherwise in one piece. The management, in a radical fit of touching kindness, gave him the rest of the day off – provided he turned up for work at the usual time next morning!

The old Midleton Distillery would probably have continued in its present form had Cork Distilleries Co, in 1966, not decided to join forces with their Dublin opposition John Jameson and John Power to form the Irish Distillers Group. The new company agreed that an all-purpose pot and column still needed to be built and Midleton had the space for this development on available and cheaper ground whereas the Dublin distilleries, hemmed in close to the city centre, had little or no room to expand. They could also raise cash by selling off some of the city property.

As the new plant took shape, the making of whiskey continued as usual at Midleton as if nothing was happening. One evening in July 1975 the men clocked off as usual from the old distillery. The following morning they returned, but instead of entering the old, historic buildings, they walked on a further few hundred yards and began producing the first make from the brand new stills.

Their environment couldn't have been much more different. Their old place of work had been an 18th-century building steeped in tradition where the smell of grist and spirit was as much a part of the structure as the bricks and mortar. Now they were entering a distillery from a different age. From the outside it could have been a factory which made dog food or processed plastics. There was no sense of tradition, no looking back at the past. It was designed for the specific purpose of making the stuff which would bring high quality Irish whiskey back to the forefront of the world spirit market as efficiently as possible.

There were no goodbyes from the men for the old plant; no closing or opening ceremonies; it was just part of a day's work. Though for present Head Distiller, Barry Crockett, it had to be a wrench. He was actually born in one of the Georgian buildings within the original distillery.

The tools with which they were making the whiskey were markedly different and with the

Above
The splendid
Georgian
buildings at
Midleton house
the distillery's
original stills.

closing of the old Midleton Distillery came the end of another era in Irish whiskey-making. Until the day it closed old Midleton made their whisky (sic) using between 5-7 per cent oats in the grist, the last distillery in Ireland to carry out this ancient tradition. The new distillery did not cater for oats at all and replaced it with unmalted barley. Otherwise, the way whiskey was made stayed

almost the same. The stillhouse was, and still is, a truly extraordinary sight to behold. The stillhouse at the old building was cramped and divided into two sections with the giant wash still awarded more or less a room of its own. At the new Midleton the pot stills, sharing the same great hall as the grain stills, were not the traditional bulbous affairs like their predecessors and also those once found at Power's, Tullamore, Royal Irish and the like. These stills were of the squatter swan-necked style preferred in Scotland and at Bushmills. The new stills at Midleton are smaller than old Irish pot stills, yet bigger than anything in Scotland. As you stand beside them, dwarfed by their bulk and height, you are reminded more of grazing brontosauruses rather than graceful swans.

Another feature is the wash backs. Once made of wood, at the new complex they are stainless steel affairs built in such a manner that they actually form the outer walls of the buildings. This is curious, because the wash is then subject to a variance in outside temperatures, which theoretically could effect the brewing process; all part of Midleton's idiosyncratic distilling style.

But what of the other distilleries which made up the Cork Distilleries Company? Since 1920 Midleton has been distilling pot still whiskey alone. In that year the North Mall Distillery was wrecked by fire and never distilled again. It was a sad loss: the distillery was one of Ireland's oldest, built in 1779 on an island, once the home of an old Dominican Friary.

Some of the buildings did survive the inferno, and in one of them some of their smaller brands of whiskeys, like Midleton Very Rare and Hewitts are today blended. Indeed, one of the vats in which the blending is carried out is over 100 years old, dating back to when North Mall was one of the most impressive sites in the glorious city of Cork. As well as the blending being carried out there,

there is also a bottling plant, which was installed in 1964.

Another of the buildings which survives is the house once lived in by the owners of the distillery, the Wise family. The family died out with bachelor Francis Wise, a noted miser, who built false walls onto the outside of the property to give visitors the appearance that he lived in a grander house than he actually did.

Elsewhere in Cork are the remains of the Watercourse Distillery (*see Hewitts*), and although The Green Distillery was reopened to make gin and Vodka for the company until the 1970s, with the advent of Midleton, whose column stills now carry out that task, The Green and John Street are now gone, leaving only the old distillery at Midleton for Irish whiskey lovers to gaze upon and lovingly admire.

MIDLETON VERY RARE

It is rare to chart the full evolution of an Irish whiskey, but with Midleton Very Rare it is possible. In hotels and pubs throughout Ireland the odd bottle of Midleton VR can be found either on the whiskey shelf or languishing deep in the cellar. If you do come across bottlings of VR, you may be able to sample each vintage over a period of time.

When it was launched in 1984 it contained not only the whiskeys which have developed since Midleton's opening in 1975, but to give some extra depth, a few casks from the old Midleton

Distillery. For blender Barry Walsh, working on Midleton Very Rare has been a learning curve. As each year passed he discovered more and more about what the whiskey was capable of achieving during maturation. This fact is reflected in the styles of the whiskeys bottled between 1984 and now. The earlier bottlings did not hang together too well with the grain not really gelling with the pot still. On reflection it seems a pity the Midleton used from the original distillery was not bottled on its own. Still, the intention was honourable.

However, over the years there have been noticeable changes. There is obviously less grain now in comparison to the brand's infancy and instead of putting together casks which appeared to fit the bill, special casks are now put to one side exclusively to make up Midleton VR. These casks are called B1s, which are bourbon casks fresh from the USA. The whiskeys now used range from 12-year-olds to 1976s and the Midleton VR of today is a very fine drink, indeed.

It remains highly exclusive and rather expensive. Only between 600 and 1,200 cases are sold each year and it enjoys a worldwide market.

TASTING NOTES MIDLETON **VR 1984**

NOSE: Velvety soft and nothing like the pot still character one might have expected. There is malt, but Highland in style, leaving the grain to steal the show. Some nutmeg essence does give a little character.

TASTE: Very sweet, very soft and very grainy. Hardly any middle or backbone to this at all.

FINISH: Bitter off-notes cling to the palate and fade reluctantly. Some malt and toffee lurking, but this doesn't get a look-in against such a strong grain imbalance.

COMMENTS: Disappointing to say the least. No balance here and the metallic finish ruins it completely.

TASTING NOTES MIDLETON **VR 1985**

NOSE A nudge on from the '84 vintage thanks to a better defined malt presence and a tell-tale harshness of unmalted barley. Still sweet but some oiliness in there, too. A gentle bourbon character is quite fruity and there are some roasted nuts lurking about also. Much more complex than its predecessor.

TASTE A pretty decent start: medium-bodied and oily with a nutty maltiness. The middle is still a little thin, though.

FINISH This starts well enough with a spiciness which wasn't around for the '84. But again the grain is rather bitter and overpowering at the very end. Not as forbidding as the previous vintage, but still far too hostile.

COMMENTS A great improvement on the first attempt. Much better balanced but the finish is still letting the side down a little.

TASTING NOTES MIDLETON VR 1986

NOSE Now starting to become quite heavy with an emphatic pot still/fruit character which takes over, whereas the ex-bourbon had previously held sway. If I didn't have it from the horse's mouth that this didn't have any sherry, I would swear it had.

TASTE Sweet start and immediately spicy. The pot still maltiness takes much longer to make its mark. Very rich, indeed.

FINISH The malt now comes into its own, but halfway through this rather long finale the grain makes its first noticeable appearance which just brings the quality down a peg or two.

COMMENTS An altogether richer whiskey than in previous years. At last it is beginning to form a character of its own and is becoming quite impressive.

TASTING NOTES MIDLETON VR 1987

NOSE The closest thing to consistency yet. Very much like the '86 but with a tell-tale mustiness making this not quite as well balanced.

TASTE Again sweet, but the sweetness doesn't linger quite so long and the spiciness nips in very fast indeed. There is a change: a trace of menthol, or something equally cooling appears on the palate.

FINISH Some woody notes muscle in quite quickly here to give a lop-sided thinness with none of the lush character of the previous year. However, like cavalry charging to the rescue, some very powerful pot still comes through at the finish to give some last minute, high quality relief to this vintage.

COMMENTS Quite a complex whiskey, not overly satisfying in some places, but delightful in others. The injury-time pot still is a cracker, though.

TASTING NOTES Midleton VR 1988

NOSE The character now has been pulled away from a fruity influence. The pot still is the sharpest yet. Rather uncluttered, striking and simple. Oh, and a touch of honey and mint make a surprising but very low-key entrance.

TASTE The very sweet start of old is gone; a shrill pot still hardness whistles about the tastebuds followed by a bourbon-cask induced spiciness. It's so busy that at no time does it settle to allow a recognisable middle to be formed.

FINISH Still sweet now and the pot still maltiness battles it out with some grain which is in pretty good nick. A dryness arrives, but takes its time about it.

COMMENTS A tangible link here between the 1988 and 1993. Showing the very first signs of becoming the Midleton Very Rare we know today.

TASTING NOTES Midleton VR 1989

NOSE Citrussy and spicy, the malt is hard chiselled into the overall character. The pot still is quite formidable, as well.

TASTE The best start yet. It begins like pure pot still; very vivid in the mouth and filling every last crevice. But for the first time in a few years the grain makes an early entrance. Having said that, they sit by each other well.

FINISH Very hard and brittle, the unmalted barley is particularly noticeable here: you feel you could almost crunch your teeth on it. Quite extraordinary.

COMMENTS In some ways I think this is the best yet, but it still does not have quite the balance which the latter-day vintages exude with their wonderful spiciness.

TASTING NOTES MIDLETON VR 1990

NOSE Carrying on where the '89 left off. Perhaps the hard pot still does not drill itself quite so far into your sinuses: this is more of a masseuse, gently caressing the senses.

TASTE Solid pot still again. There is a pattern now: pot still first, sweeter maltier notes second, pleasant grains third and somewhere, imperceptibly, warming spices fill in the gaps.

FINISH Very long and almost like a Redbreast in its pot still intensity. The bourbon wood used does add that now familiar spiciness for the very first time. Truly astounding whiskey: if you come across it, you must sample it.

TASTING NOTES MIDLETON VR 1991

NOSE Much softer and far less ebullient than the last couple of vintages. Malty but with limited complexity. Not quite boring, but not far off from it, either.

TASTE Makes amends on the palate, but again we are back to sweetness first then low-key pot still flavour following. In its favour it is a honeyed sweetness and the overall feel is beautifully lush.

FINISH Disappointing compared to previous years. The lack of pot still dominance means that the grain has a larger say than it ought. In this case it's not particularly interesting.

COMMENTS The one blip over recent years. More like an '87 or '85 than one of the brave new pot still vintages which has made this such an outstanding Irish whiskey. Worth tasting in an hotel, but don't bother with a bottle.

TASTING NOTES Midleton VR 1992

NOSE Different to any previous; a spiciness dominates for the first time. Not a million miles off the 1985, but cleaner, with more pot still and cloves?

TASTE Very rich and full-bodied. An oily start and middle. Clinging to it is a pot still deliciousness mixed with the right amount of warming, tingling spice which gves it a sweet counterbalance.

FINISH Very long, intense malt and hardly any trace of grain until the very last notes come through and hit the back of the roof of the mouth with a metallic thud. Superb.

COMMENTS A real fun whiskey last thing at night.

TASTING NOTES Midleton VR 1993

NOSE Some real pot still character bubbles proudly through. There is also an impressive sub-strata of honey and pepper and some very faint and inexplicable sherry-type fruitiness.

TASTE Dry start, the harshness of the pot still grabs the tastebuds and dominates. The malt is also strong and holds together the pot still/bourbon cask middle.

FINISH Very long and malty with some spiciness but it is the very high quality, malty Irish pot still which wins the day.

COMMENTS This is the 10th bottling of Midleton Very Rare and is scarcely recognisable from the disappointing whiskey which began it all in 1984. Now there is real pot still character and it noses and tastes like a whiskey made at Midleton. It is better than the '92: it's less spicy, perhaps, but the overall complexity is quite beguiling. It's big, brash and beautiful.

TASTING NOTES Midleton VR 1994

NOSE The pot still character of the '93 has been continued, this time with a shade more honey (and ginger?) at the expense of the peppers. One of the softer noses of the '90s but far more complex and alluring than the '91.

TASTE Sweet honey is there from the off and stays in place as the expected diamond-hard charge of the pot still arrives on cue, though with a hint of orange in tow. A little malt turns up and appears to keep out any feeling of age. It also boasts an extraordinary, liqueur-type viscousness from the very start which simply refuses to fade until the end.

FINISH Starts oily and honey-melon sweet with traces of the unmalted barley keeping a watch from the roof of the mouth. Some oaky vanilla does make it through to dry things out a little.

COMMENTS The amazing lushness is unlike any other VR produced thus far: a genuine and pleasant shock to the system. The dryness which marked the '93 vintage has been wiped out. Liqueur lovers will be delighted. VR connoisseurs may be shocked and disapprove. I, for one, am grateful that an entirely different type of Irish has been created. One, it has to be said, that is not a million miles from the 1964 Midleton which they bottled recently under the Dungourney label.

TASTING NOTES Midleton VR 1995

NOSE Since Midleton VR began life in 1984, this, of all noses, is the closest to its previous vintage. The absolutely delightful pure pot still is not quite so sharp or honeyed but is there in force. This time there is lavender where the ginger had been. A little tamer and more musty than its predecessor, but fractionally so.

TASTE Almost liqueurish in its sweet, rich, heavy-bodied, sugary start. Then an odd thing happens: the sweetness vanishes entirely as more brooding, darker characteristics take control. This seems to hang on a vanilla theme with slightly tart, stewed apple and spices in close proximity. The middle is dominated by a very hard pot still. This is about as chewable a whiskey as you can get.

FINISH Slightly bitter but this is the tail end of the pure pot still. There is also a hint of treacle toffee and a light roast Java coffee. Some oaky vanillas make themselves known at the very death.

COMMENTS The texture on the palate is such that you feel that you could stand a fork in it. This is awesome whiskey: not just because of the intensity of the flavours it conjures but because of the number of them. The 1994 version was pretty mould-busting as far as depth and lushness was concerned. This has eclipsed that and redefined the perception of Irish whiskey. Astonishing.

MILLAR'S SPECIAL RESERVE

Dublin's original Millar whisky company, located as it was close by the famous old Guinness brewery, dated back to 1843. Their Black Label brand vanished in the mid 1960s, only to re-emerge as a Cooley whiskey in time for Christmas 1994. However, Millar's Black Label was just the kind of name to give the owners of a certain world-famous blended Scotch with a very similar title palpitations. So Cooley thought again and re-

TASTING NOTES MILLAR'S SPECIAL RESERVE

NOSE Often the blends direct from Cooley under their own steam can be detected by a low-key presence of sherry on the nose. This has it, the sweet grape joining forces with the grain to offer a lush sweetness alongside the harder, oakier grains.

TASTE A busy, fruity start on the palate offers some limited sweetness before the malt gives way to a firm, dry grain.

FINISH Hots up a little as the vanilla and oak dry out. The faintest hint of coffee lingers as first a bitterness then a molasses sweetness takes grip. The surprisingly long finish ends with some pretty dry oak and bitter chocolate. Impressive.

COMMENTS Decent stuff, with limited but attractive complexity. When tasting blind I have always mistaken it for an attractive 4-year-old Scotch. The finish in particular is out of the top drawer. By comparison, the short-lived Millar's Black Label, which is the same blend only under a less contentious name, yielded far stronger sherry on the nose than Special Reserve and held the malt firmer in the middle. However, in common with most early Cooley blends, although more up-front in its flavour profile, the latter blends hold a better balance with deeper, more complex notes and almost inevitably a far better finish.

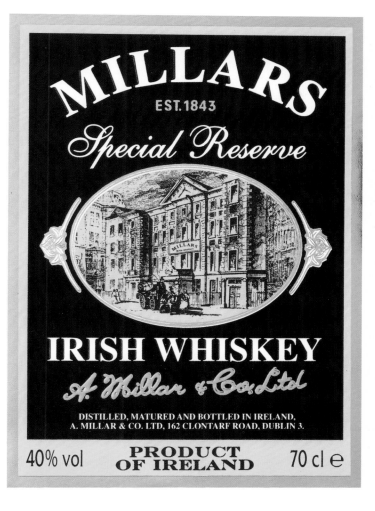

launched Black Label in early 1996 as Millar's Special Reserve. Today it can be found in Ireland, Threshers in the UK, Sweden, the Netherlands and the Benelux countries. As Cooley blends go, this one is rather unusual because 80 per cent of the grain used in the blend was sourced from sherry-treated casks.

MURPHY'S

Designed for the Irish market and distributed by Fitzgerald Wine Importers. Half of the whiskey consists of 10-year-old malt made by Irish Distillers and supplemented by both three and four-year-old grains.

TASTING NOTES Murphy's

NOSE Delicate and lively with big, fresh malty notes. The grain is also highly impressive, giving an even softness. There is more lurking about as well. If I didn't know better I would say there was something smoky, vaguely kippery - peaty, even. No. Can't be. But there is a spicy buzz to add to the intrigue.

TASTE Absolutely first-rate start with loads of malt in there at the very front offering dark fudge and then softer caramel. In the shadows is the constant presence of the grain, but keeping a discreet distance. The middle is intense with a gradual build up of spice and vanilla and the merest hint of blackberry.

FINISH Still this baffling hint of smoke hangs on. Low key grains which had taken a back seat while the malt had its fun early on arrive to ensure a sweet and dignified send off.

COMMENTS This really is a very enjoyable blend possessing admirable finesse. There is definitely a smoky presence that adds a delightful extra tang and unusual depth.

O'BRIEN'S

The last of a plethora of own label Irish whiskeys produced by Cooley in 1996 before the Christmas rush. Most are very similar in design and this, found in the Irish O'Brien off-licence chain is no exception. Designed to be a very close relative to Golden Irish with just a shade less malt.

TASTING NOTES

NOSE Very clean and attractive; light in Cooley's fashion but with just enough malt to give a honeyed tinge.

TASTE The bitterish grain start reveals itself from the very first moment and though fat and full enough to enjoy enough character to make for a pleasant whiskey, holds back the sweetening malt just too long to ensure balance.

FINISH Grainy and slightly austere. Some buttery notes at the finish add to the vanilla.

COMMENT Not one of my favourites from Cooley by any means. It is another in that frustrating area between just too austere and easy to criticise and having just enough richness of character to make for a pleasantish drink.

O'CONNELL'S

When is an Irish whiskey not an Irish whiskey? When it is called O'Connell's. Because this is a very odd Irish whiskey. Perhaps stung by Cooley's success in producing value for money whiskey, Irish Distillers were determined to prove that they could do something similar price-wise but of better quality. So in 1995 they made up a value for money blend consisting of relatively high proportions of six-year-old pure Midleton pot still and malt and lower than normal proportions of three-year-old grain. A few bottles were produced, but they never saw the light of day. Despite it being their most obscure whiskey, they entered it into the 1996 International Wine and Spirit

Competition. It was thought that by the time the competition was over it would be on the market. It wasn't. And to the astonishment of everyone at Irish Distillers, it picked up a coveted Gold Medal alongside the likes of The Glenlivet 18-year-old and Royal Salute 21-year-old. At the time of writing, the gold-gonged whiskey had still not been marketed as a commercial brand by Irish Distillers, either under their own steam or through the auspices of a supermarket or off-licence chain, though doubtless it will happen.

TASTING NOTES O'Connell's

NOSE Unmistakably Irish. And what makes this so attractive is that all three components of the blend makes their mark with some gusto. The pot still is easily the most noticeable. Those striking notes of unmalted barley, which appear hard, honeyed and fruity, give the nose a rigid shape softened by the malt lurking on a sub stratum. The grain is also evident in the guise of a more neutral spirityness which leaves you in no doubt that this is a blend. Quite beautiful.

TASTE The initial impact on the mouth points directly to a healthy input by the pot still whiskey. Like the nose it is firm and rigid with hints of sweetness. The malt offers a little toffee to chew on as well.

FINISH Mainly grain dominant with some of that pot still hanging on. The overall effect, though, is quite hard and a touch bitter.

COMMENTS This is a flint-hard, unyielding whiskey of great Irish character. There is attractive flavour development but all controlled and at no time does it ever soften in the mouth and spread with relaxed assurance over the palate. But as for it being a Gold Medal whiskey? If this is a gold, the metal to award the latest Jameson blends has yet to be discovered.

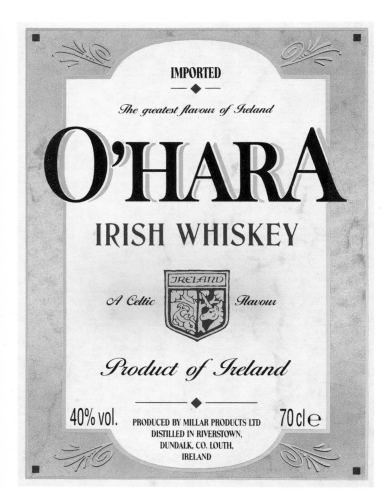

IMPORTED

The greatest flavour of Ireland

O'HARA

IRISH WHISKEY

IRELAND

A Celtic   Flavour

Product of Ireland

40% vol.   70 cl e

PRODUCED BY MILLAR PRODUCTS LTD
DISTILLED IN RIVERSTOWN,
DUNDALK, CO. LOUTH,
IRELAND

O'Hara

When introduced in early 1995, this was the first Irish blend to be made especially for a supermarket on mainland Europe. The whiskey can be found throughout France at the Intermarche chain. This blend contains around 25 per cent malt, perhaps above the norm for a supermarket Irish, with both grain and malt having been matured exclusively in bourbon casks.

TASTING NOTES O'Hara

NOSE One of the most attractive of the Cooley light blends; the malt actually stands outside to give the aroma peaks and troughs, with the grain soft and very yielding a little way below.

TASTE A rip-roaring and unsynchronized start with the grain thudding hard against the tastebuds. This is hot stuff, the spiciest Cooley has to offer. There is hope when a malty sweetness dives in; but it dives quickly out again to leave some bitter grains.

FINISH Unremittingly spicy with lots of vanilla. Very dry.

COMMENTS If you are looking for a typical soft Irish that wouldn't say boo to a goose, this is a whiskey that doesn't work too well. The bitterness is just a little too much to handle and there is insufficient support from the malt. Not one of Cooley's finest, which is a shame because it is a lot more ragged now than when it first hit the streets. The first vatting was much softer with even a touch of honey, although the finish was even then poor and pretty uncompromising. Having said that, there is another way of looking at it. If you want a whiskey to knock you about a bit and bring some life back into weary bones, this is it! Not a whiskey for the connoisseur or perfectionist and when I'm in a gentle mood I cannot take the stuff. When feeling a little under the weather or in need of a shot in the arm, this does nicely and I enjoy its fighting spirit.

OLD DUBLIN

Launched in 1995 the original dour blue label has already been changed to something more stylish and I feel the whiskey has changed somewhat from its earliest days, too. Currently the whiskey consists of some pretty basic stuff: a mixture of Midleton and Bushmills malt whiskey, though aged to about 6 years to give some depth and some younger grains. A VFM (value for money) whiskey which is available from many retail outlets throughout the UK.

TASTING NOTES OLD DUBLIN

NOSE Crisp, clean and sweetish. The malt pot still is in fruity evidence but kept in control by some pretty un-shy grain. Highly attractive with some malt coming through as well.

TASTE The grain is by far the biggest beast here. It is so overwhelming that the malt and barley have to wait a long to time arrive. When it does there is a platform of oily grain to help it along. But there is a certain lack of balance.

FINISH Long, extremely grainy with lots of delicious cocoa notes. Impressive and more-ish.

COMMENTS Of the new boys to have come from the Midleton fold, this is something of a black sheep. It has been designed to battle it out in the basement of the whiskey price range and it shows. The nose is great, though, and the finish is impressive. I'm still to be convinced about what goes on in the middle. Oddly, it has changed significantly in style in the short time of its existence. The nose is better now than the early days when the grain was completely dominant. But the old, lighter style, though more heavily grained, just seemed to sit better on the palate. The finish is superb.

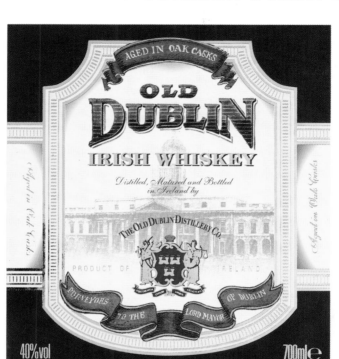

AGED IN OAK CASKS

OLD DUBLIN
IRISH WHISKEY

Distilled, Matured and Bottled in Ireland by

THE OLD DUBLIN DISTILLERY CO.

PRODUCT OF · IRELAND

PURVEYORS · TO THE · LORD MAYOR · OF DUBLIN

40%vol   700ml e

OLD KILKENNY

This is Asda's offering to the British supermarket own label Irish range. In August 1996 the idea of Asda having their own Irish was little more than a twinkle in a spirit buyer's eye; by Christmas 1996 it was already on the shelves to meet the seasonal rush. Young Midleton grain and slightly older Midleton pot still are in use here as Irish Distillers take on Cooley head to head for the first time in the battle of the British supermarket's own label.

181

TASTING NOTES

NOSE One of the heavier noses offered by a British supermarket chain, the jaunty pot still making its mark alongside toffee-caramel and some almost Canadian-style grain. There is reasonable depth.

TASTE Very sweet, silky start with caramel and the firmness of the pot still quite noticeable. The middle flattens out as the drier grain begins to take control. There is good weight and an impressive mouth-feel throughout.

FINISH Dry at first as the grain holds total domination though there is a hint of vanilla as it softens and sweetens a little for a medium-length cracker-light ultra-soft finish.

COMMENTS Not exactly a whiskey to set the world alight or an Irish to underline the point that this is a genre all its own. But as supermarket blends go - indeed, as Irish blends go - not bad at all with the pot still ensuring a degree of extra complexity. The sweetness is bound to appeal across the board and the lightness of the finish may not be exactly one for the connoisseur, but is delicate and fragile in a way that is quite appealing, even charming. I can't help thinking, though, that of all the Irish whiskeys I have ever tasted, this is the closest to a Canadian I have come across.

Old Midleton

Whiskey and storytelling go hand in hand in Ireland. And of all the Irish whiskeys to be found today this has one of the best stories attached. Midleton whisky from the original old distillery has become as rare as hen's teeth. And this fact was not lost on Sandy Ross, the man who experienced being blown stark naked through the air after standing next to an exploding pot still. His story is told in my section on Midleton. He survived the effects of the explosion well enough to become distillery manager there. In 1980, some time after his retirement, he was shown a 5-gallon stone jar of Midleton collecting dust in the cellar of a Tipperary pub. These stone demijohns were well enough known during the 1950s and 1960s and were supplied to special customers complete with wicker baskets. The whiskey filled into these jars was normally a minimum 10 years old but there was no date of distillation on the crock and the landlord had no idea it had been sitting there, but at least since 1970...three years before the old distillery closed. Sandy bought the stone jar and its precious contents and kept it at home where it stayed untouched. In 1994 Sandy's son sold the whiskey to Milroy's whiskey shop in Soho, who in turn sold it on to the legendary Irish pub nearby, The Toucan. It was decided to bottle the Midleton, and thoughtfully the label called it Midleton Whisky, spelling it the original Cork way before Irish Distillers brought it into line by adding an "e". The five-gallon jar yielded a mere

TASTING NOTES OLD MIDLETON

NOSE Sensational: this makes the hairs on the back of my neck stand up when I nose it. Massive pot still character with the unmalted barley forming a firm counter to the softer toffee and malts that are drifting about. About as perfectly balanced, especially when weighed down with lingering oils, as you can wish for.

TASTE Fat, oily, creamy start then zap: the pot still hardness kicks in with a magnificent follow through of rich cream toffee and malt.

FINISH Long, flowing malt and spice. The hard unmalted barley is still there but blends in as the softest vanilla arrives with late oak.

COMMENTS It is unlikely you will find this sold by the bottle, but you might find it on a pub bar. Whatever they charge a measure, save up and invest in one glass. This is astonishing whiskey, glorying in the oily beauty of the old wash still.

33 bottles, of which only a half a dozen or so are left for sale at Milroy's for the tidy sum of £395 per bottle. If you can't quite find that kind of cash, you can always trot around to The Toucan where you can buy it at £25 a measure.

O'NEILL'S

Irish is in. Certainly in Great Britain, anyway, where there has been an unprecedented outbreak of Irish beers and stouts finding their way onto pub pump clips, healthily backed by advertising. A natural off-shoot from this has been the rise of the Irish theme pub; basic, wooden-pewed, olde

worlde bars offering a degree of camaraderie and *craic* far removed from the usual youth culture and iced lager poverty of expectation. O'Neill's is the 67 strong – and ever growing – pub chain created by the giant British brewers Bass who go a step further in authenticity by making sure their managers are actually Irish. Their choice of established Irish whiskeys was already reasonable and a good outlet to find the brands rarely located outside the Republic itself. The fact that they introduced their own blend during 1996 is an added bonus.

This is from the Invergordon stable, using the normal grainy formula of Cooley whiskeys.

TASTING NOTES O'NEILL'S

NOSE Aromatic and characterful despite its lightness. There is even a hint of juniper fitting snugly beside the diced orange peel, caramel and cut grass.

TASTE Mouthwatering beginnings with some very sharp malt and citrus notes. There is also a mealy sweetness which hangs together attractively with some buttery oiliness.

FINISH This is where the grain comes out to play. The butter-corn sweetness disappears as the more bitter grain takes hold. The vanilla ensures a degree of austerity.

COMMENTS Of Cooley's blends this has bigger than most complexity on the nose and early start on the palate. Nothing, though, is perfect and the finish doesn't quite match up to the beauty of before. That said, this is a really tasty Irish whiskey with the closest match in character to an old, traditional Irish pot still full of unmalted barley. Yet it is simply single malt and single grain. Spooky.

PADDY

There is something about the way Paddy whiskey was so named, that you can't help feeling it could only happen in Ireland. During the 1920s and '30s there were two whiskeys which could be easily bought by the bottle. The first and most popular was Power's Gold Label. The second was Cork Distilleries Company Old Irish Whiskey, which, as good as it might have been when it slipped down the throat, was not the easiest brand name to trip off the tongue.

In the counties which made up the south-west region, collectively called Munster, Cork Distilleries had a sales rep of some repute, Paddy Flaherty. He would breeze into town on his bike, and as he did so men would scamper into the bar to be there to greet him. It was a well-known fact that if you were in close proximity as he ordered his glass, this most generous and gregarious of fellows would stand you a round.

It was his way of making sure everyone got a taste for the whiskey and put pressure on the publicans to always have some in stock. If they were running low or, heaven forbid, had actually run out, they would ring or more likely write to the distillery asking for another case of "Paddy Flaherty's whiskey".

It did not take long for Cork Distilleries to realise they were onto a winner here. Firstly, they put the name Paddy Flaherty at the foot of the label to show it was, indeed, the real stuff. Then, by degree, the label altered until they went the

whole hog and decided to call it, quite simply, Paddy. Unfortunately the company did not go as far as to give their number one salesman a bonus or a percentage of the profits they were reaping. By the time he retired from the company he was just another employee.

Of all Ireland's major pot still brands, this was the only one which didn't have to change distilleries when the Irish Distillers Group was formed. But where the whiskey is so markedly different from Paddy Flaherty's day, is that it is now no longer pot still but a blend of pot still and grain, with the blender going easy on the pot still fraction to ensure a very light whiskey.

It is one of the softest of all Ireland's whiskeys. This is because there is relatively little pot still content, but instead the grain works in tandem with single malts from both Midleton and Bushmills to keep any distinctive pot still flavour subdued. At Midleton three different types of pure malt whiskey are produced and Paddy uses the

TASTING NOTES PADDY

NOSE Not only is this a grainy nose, it also has an unusual astringent severity for Irish blended whiskey. Best when very well warmed in the hand. Even then it keeps rather too firm a grip on the pot still. Some sherried fruitiness does come through, though, with a hint of apples, as well.

TASTE Again it is the grain making the first move. It is quite soft and sweet and mild enough to allow the merest hint of pot still to follow through.

FINISH There is no trace of pot still at all as soon as the middle is passed. The grain starts quite attractively at first, keeping its sweetness in shape. But as it dries, a bitterness descends which hangs about to the very finish.

COMMENTS This whiskey does have its merits which is mainly a soft relaxed mood which is crushed by the grain towards the end. But my taste is for pot still character, of which this has very little. If you like your whiskey strong-tasting, give this a miss. If you prefer yours light and rather simplistic, then Paddy's yer maun.

very lightest of them all. Of the three whiskey codes, grain makes up the highest proportion of the blend followed by pot still and then the pure malt. But if you add up the pure malt and pot still, these outweigh the grain content.

POWER'S DISTILLERY

There are few more charming cities to visit than Dublin and an architectural exploration of its winding back streets and substantial main roads offers surprise upon surprise. But none more so for the whiskey-lover than when you cross the Liffey by the Father Mathew Bridge, pass by The Brazen Head, Dublin's oldest pub, and turn right into John's Lane. Before your disbelieving eyes is one of the most extraordinary, and to some, saddest sights, in all Ireland.

Exposed to chill winds and lashing rain by winter and having basked in the summer sun, are three pot stills which were, according to Alfred Barnard in 1887 "as bright and keen as burnished gold", but are now faded and a lifeless green. They jut proudly from a brick dais to form a bizarre silhouette against Christchurch Cathedral, which, higher up the hill, looks down upon the sight with a melancholy gothic beauty.

You have just stumbled upon the remains of the demolished stillhouse of the fabled John's Lane Distillery, for nearly two centuries the home of John Power & Son. Fortunately much of the structure has survived, but today produces artists and sculptors rather than Ireland's most cherished

whiteey since it is now the National College of Art and Design.

The famous facade, once known as the Counting House, is unchanged and each detail of illustration in Barnard's book can be accounted for. But not since 1976 has the sweet smell of mashing grist hovered on the winds above the distillery. That was when the final curtain came down on distilling in Dublin – Power had followed in the footsteps of its great rival across the river, Jameson, so that both their whiskeys began to be made from the same brand new pots and columns at Midleton.

It is unlikely that James Power, a coaching innkeeper of Thomas Street (from where the mails

Above
The Power's white label was used by independent bottlers. The famous gold label was reserved for Power's bottled at John's Lane.

Left
Bottles and casks of Power's are readied for shipping out from the John's Lane Distillery in Dublin early in the 20th century.

were sent to the north and west of the country), could have foreseen the success of his venture when he founded his tiny distillery in 1791 by converting the hostelry. His son John had teamed up with him around the turn of the century by which time he had expanded and moved premises just a few hundred yards to John's Lane. Although the business was called James Power and Son in 1804, by 1809 the venture had become a limited company under the name John Power while James remained in charge. Growth was steady until 1823 and then rapid. That happened to be the year when the laws regarding distilling were changed and made life a lot easier for whisk(e)y makers operating legally in both Scotland and Ireland.

In 1823, John Power boasted a 500-gallon still, a fair size for its day, with an annual output of 33,000 gallons – quite an increase from his father's fledgling 6,000-gallon output. But 10 years later, with the aid of even larger stills, production had increased ten-fold and Power's whiskey had arrived in the big time, and has never looked back.

Such success brought wealth and all its glorious trappings and the Power family rose within a generation from innkeepers and speculative distillers to members of Dublin high society. John Power was knighted and later became High Sheriff of Dublin. Such was his standing in the community that it was he who laid the foundation stone for the O'Connell Monument.

Meanwhile the phenomenal growth of the distillery continued. In James Power's time the original distillery was small enough to be powered by horse mill. Within half a century enough money had been found for massive expansion, not just for the materials and apparatus to make ever increasing amounts of Power's, but also for the storage capacity it required for maturation.

In 1871 the distillery was rebuilt to a classic, Victorian factory style and the lands it occupied covered nearly seven acres stretching from Thomas Street to the Quay. It had become one of the most impressive sights in central Dublin and a vital part of the economy, employing 300 people and bringing cash into the city from a wide market.

There were two central reasons for Power's impressive empire. The first was the quality of their whiskey. Even Barnard, who gave chapter and verse on every nut and bolt that made a distillery work but was loathe to offer detail or opinion of the whiskey it made, was moved to comment: "We had previously sampled the firm's make of 1885, which we thought good and most useful, either as a blending or single whisky (sic). The old make, which we drank with our luncheon, was delicious, and finer than anything we had hitherto tasted. It was as perfect in flavour, and as pronounced in the ancient aroma of Irish Whisky (sic) so dear to the hearts of connoisseurs, as one could possibly desire, and we found a small flask of it very useful afterwards on our travels."

The other was the company's unusually innovative skills. While it turned its back until relatively recently on blending its pot still whiskey

Right

Once rivals in a competitive market place, Paddy and Power's are now stable mates, owned by IDG and distilled at Midleton.

with grain, it had no such inhibitions with bottling whiskey in any shape or size that would sell. It had been common practice in Ireland for distillers to sell their whiskey by the cask to outlets that would either bottle it or sell direct from the cask. To prevent the possibility of contamination or adulteration, as well as protect their own good name, Power's bottled their own whiskey with a distinctive and now famous gold label. By then one of Ireland's largest distillers, they were nevertheless astute enough to be the first company to sell their whiskey in miniatures called Baby Power's. To achieve that notable first, new Government legislation was required. But with the Powers being so formidable a family it was no surprise that the changes to the law were made.

Such was the distillery's output that by the close of the 19th century Power's ceased floor malting and had begun buying in. Otherwise it remained a traditional pot still distillery until the 1950s when the company finally gave way to trend and installed a continuous still to make grain spirit for blending, a move which would have sent the first John Power and his son spinning in their graves! They had always been opposed to what they had seen as a fouling of their pure Irish whiskey. But in 1932, when Sir Thomas Talbot Power died, there was no one left on the board with the Power name, yet it remained in the family through his sisters. The strong family principles continued, but with Irish whiskey struggling – particularly on the export market – new avenues had to be explored. The final and most dramatic of outcomes was the merger of the company in 1966 with the other two remaining distilleries in the Irish Republic, Cork Distilleries and their greatest rivals, John Jameson & Son. It was agreed they would move lock, stock and barrel to a new distilling complex at Midleton. And at the same time they also decided to turn their famous all pot still bottled whiskey into one containing a grain distilled at John's Lane.

Typically, it was Power's, the oldest distillers in Eire, who were the last to reluctantly quit their post. It was a sad day for Dublin and Irish whiskey in particular. Today, those three massive pot stills defiantly stand their ground, as green as the Irish flag, and as impressive and proud as the whiskey they once made.

POWER'S

Just around the corner from the Midleton Distillery where Power's is made today is a very small pub, Mahoney's in Sraid Connail - O'Connell Street. The main window is massive and brightened by a gold and red logo. It reads Power's. It is a sight which jolts the system and draws the whiskey lover inside. On the shelves and optics there are several bottles of Power's whiskey and very little else. When I went in there wasn't a Jameson in sight.

The elderly owner told me she sold Power's by the crateload. Good news for Irish Distillers – or is it? Once the whiskey for the town was Paddy which was made for decades at Midleton by Cork Distilleries. Then Irish Distillers put their marketing muscle into Jameson. Yet drinkers at Mahoney's switched allegiance to Power's. The reason I was given both at the pub and during my travels in Ireland was that it was the best whiskey of the lot. I enthusiastically agree. To drink at home it is a delight; to drink in an Irish pub is one of life's simple but unforgettable pleasures.

Power's is ridiculously hard to find outside Ireland, even in the UK. Yet it is a whiskey which should always be there somewhere in the cabinet, not only to drink yourself, but with which to also entertain Irish guests, for there is no better way of making them feel at home. Power's is still the biggest seller in all Ireland and has been since they began bottling it in 1894. In those days it was pure pot still whiskey; today Midleton produces a delectable blend of pot still and grain whiskeys with an emphasis on the pot still which makes Jameson appear soft and Paddy almost feeble.

Anyone who has tasted Power's will not be surprised to learn that the make up of the pot still portion uses 60 per cent unmalted barley to 40 per cent malted barley, the highest ratio of that type produced in Midleton. And, even more significantly, the pot still goes to make up some 70 per cent of the overall blend, quite astonishing when you consider it is priced in the same bracket as Paddy and Jameson! There is no use of single malt whiskey whatsoever and the distillation method used is designed to produce the highest notes possible. This type of whiskey matures well in the cask and reacts perfectly with the wood. The end product is a whiskey which just bursts at the seams with high flavour development.

The whiskey is known both as Gold Label and Three Swallow. The former is self-explanatory, the latter has nothing to do with the birds fluttering around the bottle's neck. It is because it was said you should drink your glass of Power's not in one, but in three swallows. Sound advice, but make sure you keep it in your mouth for a good 10 to 15 seconds before it slips down your throat. Then you will see why an entire nation can't be wrong.

REDBREAST

Of the many brand names under which Jameson whiskey was found, Redbreast was for a long time one of the better known. It also acquired the epithet "The Priest's Bottle" for no matter which priest you visited, he had a bottle in the house.

TASTING NOTES Power's

NOSE The most attractive of all Irish whiskeys. First to show is a massive pot still character which is hard and striking, but this is softened, dissolved almost, by a viscous graininess. The overall effect is a stunning dovetailing of honeyed sweetness and dry, peppery tones. This spice effect comes from the wood which is also present, thanks to the grain, in a creamy vanilla, cream soda gentleness. Glorious stuff.

TASTE An immediate explosion of flavours on the palate, most of them spicy. There is a well defined pot still rigidity on which all else hangs, but those honey notes come through strongly and fuse delectably with the spice. The effect is tingling and voluptuous.

FINISH Long, sweet and sour with lingering spice. Hangs around in one form or another in different parts of the mouth for several minutes. It's mainly the spice, though, which refuses to die.

COMMENTS This is a monster of a whiskey of which the nose and tastebuds can never tire. Its very best effects can be experienced when drunk at room or pub temperature without ice or water. Once, I preferred Black Bush for all round charm and complexity, but over the last two years I think Power's has improved and familiarity has bred anything but contempt. Fresh tastings never disappoint and during 1996 it won a deserved Gold Medal at the inaugural International Spirit Challenge in London. Classic is an overused cliché in the drinks world, but if this isn't one then I'd like to know what is.

It was a brand name for Jameson's pure Irish pot still, bottled in bond by Gilbey Vintners of Ireland as a sister whiskey to their Crock of Gold brand. It began life in 1939 with Jameson filling Gilbey's own casks. Its make-up was quite simple: for every two ex-sherry casks used, there was an ex-bourbon cask tipped in, too.

The whiskey was sold almost exclusively in Ireland with only a dribble arriving in Britain. In 1968 Jameson decided to end links with the bonded trade, but Gilbey's persuaded suppliers to continue selling them pot still until 1971 when the Bow Street Distillery was closed. By the time of the last bottling in 1985, the whiskey was not quite what it once had been. Many casks aged between 22 and 25 years had to be used, giving it a tired feel. The present Redbreast was relaunched

Unique among whiskeys, Redbreast is a 'single', unblended, pure pot still Irish whiskey which has been

triple distilled and matured in oak casks for not less than twelve years.

YEARS **12** OLD

REDBREAST

PURE POT STILL

IRISH WHISKEY

Matured in Oak Casks for not less than twelve years

Fitzgerald & Co. Ltd.

40% vol. DISTILLED MATURED AND BOTTLED IN BOND FOR FITZGERALD & CO. 11-12 BOW STREET DUBLIN 7. 700 ml e

This uncompromising dedication to authenticity and quality gives Redbreast a traditional smooth mellow character

and a taste which is full flavoured and assertive but not over robust.

TASTING NOTES REDBREAST

NOSE Stupendous nose; a bit of nip and bite but the sheer brittleness of the pot still is so real and alive you feel you could snap it in two. The malt also comes through alongside an apple-like fruitiness and a hovering trace of sherry, too. Every bit as clean as the old Redbreast is musty.

TASTE Just a sip is enough to fill your mouth with a multi-layered attack of malt and pepper plus a few sherry notes with the Irish pot still character arriving on the second wave and refusing to budge. This is enormously assertive stuff.

FINISH Very long indeed, and the late spice comes as the perfect ending to the great complexity of all that has gone on before. Although there is a dryness, some honey and fudge character also makes itself known and is more dangerously delectable than any other (apart from Power's and Green Spot).

COMMENTS This is a marvellous whiskey. The pot still character gives an enormous depth and each time you taste it another facet of its make-up is spotted. A perfect after-dinner whiskey.

by Irish Distillers as their single all pot still whiskey. The heavier style of pot still is used in its vatting with whiskeys of 12 years and upwards being selected. Some sherry casks are used, but the bourbon-cask character comes through much more clearly. Still hard to find, inside or outside Ireland, it is beyond my understanding why IDG have not been shouting about this magnificent whiskey from the rooftops.

ROYAL IRISH DISTILLERY

Question: what have the downstairs bar of The Elk in Dundonald, Distillery Football Club, a park in Ulster's capital and a few bottles of 1951

Royal Irish whiskey which are still on sale, each have in common? Answer: they are all that is left of the old Dunville Distillery, one of the greatest names in Ulster if not Irish whiskey.

The history books will tell you that the Royal Irish Distillery made its last spirit in the late 1930s. But some older supporters of Distillery FC I met at their New Grosvenor Stadium at Lisburn, just outside Belfast, remember it working into the '50s, a claim backed up by a single cask of 1951 pot still found in a warehouse and now on offer in bottled form.

Dunville was for a great many years a Belfast whiskey and enjoyed a very high reputation. The family firm started off as blenders and in 1869 built Belfast's first commercial distillery just off the Grosvenor Road, and did not do the job by half. It was a massive structure, the company clearly setting their stall out as major players in the whiskey game. But to build the distillery at all the Dunville family had to carry out a bit of legal jiggery-pokery and find a loophole in the law. In those days distillers were not allowed to deal in spirits, other than their own, unless outside a two-mile radius from their distilleries. To overcome that hurdle two companies were set up: William Dunville and Co, distillers, and Dunville and Co, spirit dealers.

Even though the plant was a large one it continued to expand, winning gold medals at every exhibition it entered. It even survived the First World War, the trade war following the

Opposite
An old advertisement for Dunville's. The Elk Bar in Dundonald is a shrine filled to the brim with Dunville's memorabilia.

emergence of the Irish Free State and Prohibition in the USA, where it had previously sold well, coming out of this trilogy of setbacks in a reasonably unscathed condition.

But just as they seemed set to relaunch into the USA in the mid-1930s things started to go disastrously wrong. By that time the Dunville family connection had prematurely ended. When the elder statesman of the company, Robert Dunville died in 1910, his son, Colonel John Dunville, continued to run a tight company. He was succeeded by his eldest son, Captain Robert Dunville, but the firm was thrown into turmoil when, on a business trip to South Africa to secure further exports, Robert died. With his brother, John, having been killed during the First World War in an action for which he was posthumously awarded the Victoria Cross, there were no more Dunvilles to keep the flag flying.

The non-family board did not have the same belief in the company as the founding family. Despite having three pot stills and two grain stills, thus being self-sufficient enough to produce both blended and pure pot still whiskey, and owning the Scottish distillery at Bladnoch, Wigtownshire, they decided not to attack the American market and approached the Scottish Distillers Company Limited, inviting them to take them over. Their prospective buyers were not sufficiently interested, announcing they had no faith in Irish whiskey.

Amazingly Dunville wound themselves up, an action which shocked Belfast and has never been fully explained by industrial historians. Royal Irish Distilleries were, compared to other companies, in a healthy position. An attempt was made to produce whiskey at the old distillery again in the 1950s but this was a short-lived bid to rekindle distilling in the city.

In 1879, just nine years after the building of the distillery was completed, workers from Dunville set up their own football team on a piece of land lent to them by the distillery. The club went on to win the Irish League just 17 years later and around the turn of the century were one of the most powerful clubs in Ireland.

Apart for a short spell in the 1920s when the expanding distillery tried to build on the site of the club's ground, only to find it was unsuitable, Distillery stayed at their Grosvenor Road ground until 1971. In 1963 the side played Benfica at Windsor Park in the European Cup. The game was switched from the Distillery because a bumper crowd was expected. But in monsoon conditions, only 17,000 attended – 3,000 less than the Distillery ground capacity.

Remarkably, the part-timers of Distillery held the reigning European champions to a 3-3 draw, with Tom Finney, famous for wearing the white of England and Preston, being brought out of retirement to play his only game for the club and wear the white of Distillery FC.

The ground was literally in the shadows of the grim, four-storey high, brick-built distillery. When it was constructed it was on the outskirts of the town and from the roof a dramatic view of the city and the countryside was offered. But by 1971 it found itself at the heart of the conflict around the Grosvenor Road. Although the club was one of only a handful to draw both its supporters and players from Catholic and Protestant areas, the ground became the target of firebomb attacks. With sadness the old club moved to a green field site and another link was lost.

Recently Belfast wine and spirit merchant Philip Russell resurrected the Dunville name with Invergordon supplying a Cooley blend for the brand. His company also owns three bars, one of them The Elk. Downstairs is a glittering array of original Dunville's mirrors and adverts he has compiled over the years. *(See Dunville's).*

SAINSBURY'S

The first British supermarket chain to introduce their own Irish whiskey. Unlike those which followed, this is pure malt. And because it came from Cooley, obviously there were similarities between this and Tyrconnell. Yet since its launch for Christmas 1994, this whiskey has remained remarkably more consistent in character than Cooley's own brand. This is partly because higher percentages of original 1989 distillate is being used. The average age for the whiskey hovers somewhere between five and six years and it appears to have been a popular seller for the store. On its introduction, Sainsbury's spirit buyer was stunned to discover that it was outselling Jameson

TASTING NOTES Sainsbury's

NOSE The grassy malt is rather crisp and clipped. You don't have to be a genius to spot the lemony youth. This has many of the characteristics of an 8-year-old Speyside. Very simplistic yet attractive nonetheless.

TASTE That grassiness translates perfectly into a lively, sweet malt that attacks the palate with a refreshing cleanness.

FINISH The sweet malt shows signs of caramel as it fades and the crispness is replaced by a softly spiced chewyness. Some vanilla on the very finish but the oak is very low key.

COMMENTS This is a delicious little malt showing maturity way beyond its years. I am particularly impressed by the way it makes the mouth water. Certainly quite prim and elegant.

three to one and Cooley are still quietly delighted at how many vattings for this malt they continue having to make.

TESCO SPECIAL RESERVE

This is yet another British supermarket chain which introduced its own Irish whiskey in time for Christmas 1996. And another that is selecting its blend from a number of samples proffered by Invergordon using Cooley whiskey.

Although this is an Invergordon blend, the signature on the bottle is that of Cooley blender, Noel Sweeney.

TASTING NOTES
TESCO SPECIAL RESERVE

NOSE Disappointing, grain-soaked. Until it warms up in the hand it is just about impossible to pick out the malt, and even then offers no more than a token ear. Very vodka-spirity and warns of a possible rough attack on the palate...

TASTE Which duly arrives. There is first a well-intentioned spurt of something malty but it is soon crushed underfoot by marauding grain.

FINISH It's grain all the way. But being Cooley, this is not such a bad thing, and the bitter-sweet dark chocolate follow through is at once quite startling and absolutely delicious.

COMMENT Forget the nose. Don't waste your time looking for subtle fragrances. As for lashings of malt on the palate, look elsewhere. But the middle and finish are astounding. Cooley's grain whiskey is some of the best I have experienced. In this bottling, it is the pick of the best. It's only fault is that there is a brief nano-second you wonder if this is vodka. The magnificence of the oak finish dispels any doubts.

TULLAMORE DEW DISTILLERY

Opposite
Labels from a
bottle of
Tullamore
c. 1920.

Straddling the banks of the narrow and gentle flowing River Clodagh, in the centre of a neat and friendly Offaly town, lie the crumbling remains of a distillery which in its day was one of the great whiskey centres of Ireland.

The distillery was once Tullamore which was founded in 1829 by one Michael Molloy, taking

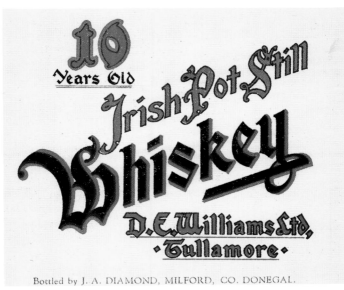

211

advantage of the closure of two other distilleries
which had earlier operated in the town. Although
a rival distillery was built soon after, Molloy's
enterprise saw off that particular threat. The
distillery, by no means the biggest in Ireland but
enjoying a fine reputation, passed into the hands
of nephew Bernard Daley in 1857, on Molloy's
death. Thirty years later it was the turn of his son,
Captain Bernard Daley to take control. But
Captain Daley decided his life lay outside the
whiskey industry and promoted the distillery's
engineer, Daniel E Williams, to the post of general
manager. Williams had been at the distillery since

he was 15 and, very much unlike his employer, whiskey was in his blood and was his whole life. After Williams took control he persuaded Captain Daley to invest in expanding the plant. As Williams grew more powerful and Captain Daley's meagre interest in the distillery withered further, he managed to buy into the company, eventually taking overall control.

The distillery had success with their pot still whiskey which they marketed as Tullamore Dew. Williams had selected the brand name as a pun on his own initials. The name had a ring which appealed, as did the style of the whiskey which was a little lighter than the average Irish pot still. The advertising slogan: "Give Every Man his Dew" became one of the best known in Ireland.

With Tullamore being located in the heart of the Irish midlands, where the roads were rutted and travel was slow and where steam was yet to arrive, the distillery thrived in its earliest days thanks to the Grand Canal which runs through the town. Coal was brought to the distillery from England and the same barges would then travel back, laden with whiskey. With the arrival of the railways, communications improved even further. However, every convenient means of transportation counts for nothing if no one is buying your product and by the 1950s Tullamore Distillery, like many others in Ireland, was experiencing financial problems. The market had shrivelled considerably and the distillers looked to new horizons to rediscover success.

Opposite
D E Williams'
old bottling
warehouse in
Tullamore.

They hit upon the idea of producing a whiskey-based liqueur which they called Irish Mist. Daniel Williams had begun the search for a recipe in his day, but it was not until after the war that they discovered it in the most unlikely of circumstances. It is said Williams had heard about a traditional Irish drink called heather wine, its principal ingredients being Irish pot still whiskey, herbs and heather honey. But his researches came to nought as it appeared the secret had been taken to the continent over a century before. Sometime in 1948 an Austrian refugee visited the head office opposite the distillery and showed them a recipe similar to the one they were hunting. And that, legend has it, is how Irish Mist came into being, although today it is made by Cantrell & Cochrane, still in Tullamore, but using Scotch whisky as well as Irish.

Oddly, the success of Irish Mist was the death knell for the old distillery which was becoming increasingly expensive to operate and in need of maintenance and upgrading. By 1954 they had more pot still whiskey than they knew what to do with and ceased production, never to start again. Parts of the distillery can still be seen, but as this book was being researched, I witnessed some of the old warehouses being demolished. Tullamore practised triple distillation and those stills can still be seen. They have moved to an outside site at the Kilbeggan distillery just down the road where they cut an impressive, though forlorn figure.

And the only dew they produce today forms on

Opposite
"Give every man his Dew", the famous old Tullamore phrase, is one of the most fondly remembered.

the outside, rather than the inside, when another morning dawns and they become an even more distant part of Irish distilling history.

TULLAMORE DEW

While this blend has been ticking over in Ireland for the last few years, abroad it has achieved success out of all proportion to the quality of the whiskey. Being very light it has made a mark with those who prefer their whiskey not to occupy the tastebuds too much.

The early days of this whiskey have already been told since they were so closely knitted to the success of the old Tullamore Distillery. But 1993 can be seen as a watershed year for this whiskey since Irish Distillers allowed it to go to Cantrell & Cochrane, a company which themselves once hoped to own the Irish Distillers Company, rather than just one of its brands. Tony O'Brien, C&C's managing director immediately announced bold plans for the brand: "We intend to quickly establish Tullamore Dew in the core Irish whiskey market of Ireland, the UK and the US and to further support it in its existing areas of strength."
It is the top-selling Irish in Germany and Denmark and is strong in France.

TULLAMORE 1948

Taken from the cask as a 42-year-old, this is one of a number of old Irish whiskeys discovered in the sample room at William Cadenhead which have recently been issued as a miniature. There were

TASTING NOTES

NOSE The grainiest, least Irish of all popular Irish whiskeys; there is a begrudging pot still maltiness, but very faint.

TASTE Soft and light to the point that it is hard to detect this as an Irish whiskey. It is very sweet from the outset and some malt does assemble for the middle. But it is simple and lacking in any form of complexity.

FINISH There is a welcome wave of spiciness which lasts only a second or two and is replaced by a buttery smoothness and heaps of vanilla.

COMMENTS An untaxing whiskey which does not excite the palate. The sweetness can be attractive. But watch this one: drink it too cold and it can be rather astringent and harsh, and following the wrong kind of food it can be bitter and unyielding. Best drunk hand-warm and with a very clear palate. Only then does it reveal a limited charm.

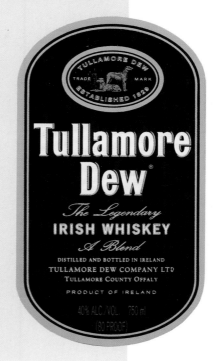

Tullamore Dew®

The Legendary
IRISH WHISKEY
A Blend

DISTILLED AND BOTTLED IN IRELAND
TULLAMORE DEW COMPANY LTD
TULLAMORE COUNTY OFFALY

PRODUCT OF IRELAND

40% ALC./VOL.   750 ml
(80 PROOF)

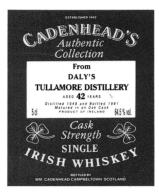

enough for 41 tiny bottles, each costing £25. Four can be found in a special boxed set also containing John's Lane, Royal Irish, Jones Road and a Tullamore '52.

TULLAMORE 1949

(65.3 per cent abv)
No-one at William Cadenhead can give me the full story of the history of this Irish whiskey. But my suspicions are that it may be

---

TASTING NOTES TULLAMORE 1948

NOSE Lots of sap and vanilla but some malty and sweet honey notes do make themselves heard above the old age static which clogs up the nosebuds. Quite attractive, as it happens.

TASTE The very first sign is one of advancing malt, but this is swept aside by lots of oak and mint. The oakiness is just about bearable and defuses a little to let in hints of pot still hardness and raisins.

FINISH Quite long and oaky with a sweetness being maintained despite the vanillins wanting to dry things out.

COMMENTS The whiskey has just about held together and is certainly drinkable. Miraculously, the pot still has managed to survive the oaky onslaught. Even so, the overall picture some minutes after you have swallowed is that you have just taken one of those milky, magnesium tablets for an upset stomach.

samples of the same splendid Tullamore that was available in full bottled form and featured elsewhere in this section. The tasting notes below are for the 214 miniatures released on the market at £20 each. I have tasted them side by side and the original sample shows some extra fruitiness, but there are a great many similarities, too.

TASTING NOTES
TULLAMORE 1949

NOSE This has a stunning nose for its age. The honey that is hinted at in the '48 vintage is here with clarity, as is the rich pot still character. There is fresh hay and just the right amount of oak to ensure balance.

TASTE The pot still, with all its juicy-fresh barley rigidity is first to show and comes through strongly. There is lashings of oily honey to add a sweetness to the sharp barley and some oakiness adds a cinnamon-like spice.

FINISH Long and very clean. The pot still unmalted barley remains the main character with a honeycomb bitter-sweetness also shining through.

COMMENTS This is magnificent whiskey, not one just to be kept in the bottle. If you ever see the miniatures, buy two. One to drink on St. Patrick's Day. The other to keep. Unlike the '48 this shows exactly what a marvellous whiskey this distillery once made. Outstandingly beautiful.

TULLAMORE 1952

Bottled by Cadenhead in 1991 there are 21 miniatures and one full bottle still surviving. Part of the rare Irish whiskeys discovered by the company but one not made aware to me by the company for my first edition of 1994. Ten of the bottles can be bought only as part of a special boxed collection of five "lost" Irish whiskeys, each costing £200 a piece.

TASTING NOTES TULLAMORE 1952

NOSE Distinct traces of exhausted wood abound; there is something faintly medicinal in a non-peaty way. The spirit also adds to an effect of polished wooden floors. But on the plus side there is something attractively herbal as well. Sweet and still a little malty, even the exhausted wood does not detract from a quirky nose.

TASTE Rather than drinking an ancient old Irish whiskey you are convinced you are sucking a throat lozenge.

FINISH Very long deep, vaguely sappy with burnt liquorice.

COMMENTS Despite all I have to say, this is not unpleasant. Though not the way I prefer to remember the old Tullamore Distillery. But from a whiskey designed for 10 years in the wood and spent 38, what do you expect?

TULLAMORE DEW 12 YEARS OLD

Developed in 1995 between whiskey makers and blenders Irish Distillers and brand owners Campbell and Cochrane, this was designed mainly for the duty free shelves where it is easily spotted. To keep the light character of the whiskey exactly the same types of whiskey are used in this as the standard Tullamore Dew. The difference here, apart from the obvious ageing, is a splash of extra pot still whiskey to give more body and weight befitting a blend of this age.

TASTING NOTES

NOSE: Just a little waspish, but the initial sting is eased by some citrus notes, unusual for a whiskey this age, and a definite presence of pot still which deflects the harsher grain notes. Rich caramel in there, too.

TASTE It's the sweet caramel first to show then some softly oaked grain and firmer pot still arrive side by side. Malt is also evident, but the grain is now coming through like a young Bourbon from the Barton Distillery.

FINISH The licks of flame that had been kept under control by the stronger notes rage as everything calms down. It is the caramel, though, which saunters through to the finish. All this sweetness is ended by the vanilla and oak.

COMMENTS In a blind nosing I'd say it was Irish. In a blind tasting I'd be confused; certainly there are Irish traits but all that toffee would convince me we had a Canadian. Whichever, this is a

different kettle of fish to the disappointing standard Tullamore Dew. Actually quite attractive, providing you are not looking for anything too challenging.

TYRCONNELL DISTILLERY

The Tyrconnell is a proud name which conjures up many different images of Ireland. The romantic among us may recall the ancient Gaelic kingdom once located in the remote north-west of Ireland by that epithet, or the sportsman may remember reading about the horse of that name which won the Irish Classic, the Queen Victoria Plate in 1876 at odds of 100-1, or, more likely today, it might just be the whiskey which comes readily to mind. In 1992 the single malt whiskey from Cooley Distillery was bottled and sold under that title for the first time. This may have been Cooley's debut, but The Tyrconnell brand was far from new. It was one of the main whiskeys made at the Derry Distillery of A A Watt (a family company which had owned the legendary horse) and was sold successfully as pure pot still in the USA.

The distillery was on the brink of closure by the early 1920s and the death of Andrew Watt, ironically the result of a hunting accident, allowed the Distillers Company Limited of Scotland to move in and buy the concern in 1922 and close it three years later. The distillery, like many others in Ireland, was also badly hit by prohibition in the States and the trade war between the new Irish Free State and the UK. The Watt family, now without a distillery, then formed a blending company which continued to market The Tyrconnell but that, too, closed in 1970.

The current Tyrconnell, with its five red stars, is a vatting of five-year-old malts. Its very first, three star bottling of three and four-year-olds (the stars were upped not to represent the years but simply give the impression of better quality whiskey inside), had been too dependent on early, experimental whiskeys and was not too pleasant. However, top Scottish blender Billy Walker of Burn Stewart Distillers had been brought in to iron out some initial distilling difficulties. On his suggestion Cooley even produced a very heavily peated Irish whiskey, which at 25 parts per million of phenols created by peat is as heavy as some Scottish island and Islay whiskies.

Today The Tyrconnell is delicious: a consistently better malt which has been vatted by legendary Scottish blender Jimmy Lang, once of Chivas Bros., who compares Cooley whiskey to a high-class Scottish Lowland malt whisky. Beware, though, the occasional old sub-standard bottling. Also beware the term used on the label "Pure Pot Still", lest you confuse it with the Redbreasts and Green Spots of this world.

To Cooley, this means produced entirely in a pot still from 100 per cent malted barley (i.e. single malt), which is technically correct but confusing in terms of Irish whiskey. In traditional terms "Pure Pot Still" means made in a copper pot but with a mixture of malted and un-malted barley (and possibly oats and/or rye). I have irritated Cooley by writing about this, but while the label remains the same, I feel duty bound to do so. It is sold in Holland, Switzerland, Northern Ireland, USA, France, Germany and the UK.

TASTING NOTES TYRCONNELL SINGLE MALT

NOSE Sometimes nosing a Tyrconnell can be like sticking your head in a bowl of fruit salad. Certainly there is diced, freshly picked apple, hints of lime, some under-ripe plums. And at the back of it all is some juicy malt, almost unripened in character, but not quite. Usually quite invigorating, though the occasional vatting may be a little flatter, perhaps even feinty. But that is rare.

TASTE A citrusy, young-malty feel is the first to make an impression. This is curious because for the first 10 seconds the whiskey manages to achieve neither sweetness nor dryness. Perhaps an indefinable complexity that hangs beautifully with some oilier notes means it achieves both with the two styles cancelling each other out until finally a sensual sweetness finds its way through. Youth, however, is the name of the game. The citrus-spice theme runs through the whiskey, the DNA trait of Cooley. Also, with the malt being light in build, some chocolate notes compensate to make for a chewable whiskey. Very attractive, indeed.

FINISH In the end this whiskey pitches towards a dry character with the oak noticeable with some tell-tale bitter chocolate notes, though this is very short-lived. Ultimately rather flat, and pretty short.

COMMENT Of all the Cooley brands, this is the one which shifts in character style most of all. It is older whiskey than when it was launched, to be sure. But I feel that the younger stuff, after initial teething problems, had more finesse and richness. Some Tyrconnell bottled in 1995 had feinty characteristics which did not appeal, but that was a one off. The present version is still enjoyable, nonetheless.

THE
TYRCONNELL
★ ★ ★ ★ ★
◆ SINGLE MALT ◆

Tyrconnell
wins!
100 to 1.

PURE POT STILL
IRISH WHISKEY
DISTILLED, MATURED AND BOTTLED IN IRELAND
ANDREW A. WATT & CO.
RIVERSTOWN, DUNDALK, IRELAND.

ESTABLISHED 1762

40% Vol.   PRODUCT OF IRELAND   70 cl ℮

TYRCONNELL LIMITED EDITION

Identical story to the Locke's Limited Edition, except here the casks - though hand picked as the best from the 1989 vintage - are possibly a shade inferior to Locke's and as a result are sold slightly more cheaply.

TASTING NOTES
TYRCONNELL LIMITED EDITION

NOSE From an aromatic point of view, this is one of the finest pure malt whiskeys to have come out of Ireland for a long time. There is full-honeyed richness to this which one would only normally find from the unmalted barley in Jameson Gold.

TASTE A very hard and crisp barley flavour one normally associates with the unmalted variety is the first to hit home. The sweetness is moderated by a genuinely mouth-watering sharpness. Medium-bodied but packed with fresh barley character, as if chewing the unripened grain.

FINISH Medium length with a build up of spices. Some orangey-citrus notes also begin to make a mark alongside some oaky tones.

COMMENTS Apart from the peated Connemara, this is the finest Cooley whiskey I have yet tasted. Whiskey of this quality makes a nonsense of Irish distillers old claims that Cooley's whiskey was poor stuff. This is glorious whiskey with a truly remarkable barley character. With a whiskey like this to accompany Connemara Cooley has reached its place among the world's truly great distilleries.

WAITROSE

A Cooley blend from Invergordon made for and sold exclusively by the British supermarket chain, Waitrose. Launched in early 1995, there is a reasonably high malt content – 30 per cent.

TASTING NOTES WAITROSE

NOSE The grain is quite bold and firm here. A dry nose with the oak quietly confident and the malt lingers just behind. Quite subtle.

TASTE Very fat and sweet start and quite a surprise after the rigidity of the nose. The creaminess holds the malt well but again it is the excellent grains which are the star of the show. There is a feel of sweetcorn that sits effectively on the palate.

FINISH Long with a sweet and dry battle at first but the drier vanillas win in the end. There is also a soft spice tingle at the very end; rather unusual for Cooley.

COMMENTS A surprise package. The nose is subtle and firm; the palate is anything but. The corn used in the grain adds a lot of character to this whiskey which is immensely easy to drink and ultimately an enjoyable Irish. Similar to Ballygeary, but just a tad weightier with the malt and sweetness adding extra depth. Despite the above supermarket average content of malt, it is the grain that dominates. If this doesn't prove that balance, which is lacking here, is more important than malt content, nothing will.

CHAPTER FIVE

POTEEN

THE WORD IN THE GLEN SAYS THERE IS PLENTY OF "THE STUFF" ABOUT JUST NOW. THE STUFF, TO THE IRISH, MEANS ONLY ONE THING: POTEEN. POTEEN OR POTEIN (BUT ALWAYS PRONOUNCED POTCH-EEN) IS AN IRISH SPIRIT.

Opposite
An illustration
from 1871 shows
an illicit distiller
selling his poteen
to grateful,
weary travellers.

It isn't whiskey anymore: not so much because it is never matured the three years required to make it so – that's the rule for Parliament whiskey – but because these days it's nearly impossible to find an illicit distiller who sticks exclusively to grain in the making of his prized, colourless fluid.

It was not too hard for me to track down a latter-day poteen-maker when I was last in Ireland. That was partly because he was as keen to talk to a real, live whiskey writer as I was to see a secret craftsman at work. These days if you want some of the "real stuff" you have to ask a friend of a friend. Sixty years ago H V Morton, whose travel writing was a cross between William Cobbett's and Michael Palin's, discovered poteen with an old man in Co. Cork who let him have some only after Morton had told him, "Mike

O'Flaherty's black cow has died on him." The asking price was nine shillings a bottle even in 1930; today it costs around seven or eight punts, sometimes even more. But at least you don't have to remember coded messages.

The poteen-maker has a very special place in the hearts of the Irish and today's proper illicit distillers, as opposed to those who mass produce very poor quality stuff by adulterating it with meths, are viewed with a national pride that goes deep into Ireland's psyche. It all began on Christmas Day, 1661 when the English-based Government slapped a tax of fourpence a gallon on all whiskey made. The number of illicit distillers increased by alarming proportions over the following centuries as the tax continued to rise and the lot of the Irish peasant worsened quite drastically.

It is all too easy to romanticise this period when a genuinely suppressed nation displayed their contempt for their lords by taking to the hills, bogs and glens to produce a whiskey which not only generated some much needed cash for its makers, but also was a welcome escape for the tens of thousands who drank it in Ireland's countless shebeens. And although poteen has earned its rightful place in Irish folklore, it was a feature of brutal times. While there was some fun and an understandable sense of achievement and victory over the authorities each time a drop from those mobile stills crossed an Irishman's lips, there was a much darker side to it as well.

The duty on a gallon of whiskey had been raised to one shilling and tuppence by 1785 and to help finance the Napoleonic Wars, it was raised again to a numbing six shillings and a penny ha'penny in 1815. It was then that illicit distillation in Ireland was at its height, and the battle against it at its most bloody.

The Government sent soldiers out to aid the Excise authorities in suppressing illicit distillation. The most extraordinary contemporary account I have been able to find sits in the Public Records Office of Northern Ireland. They are the letters of an officer in the army, Samuel Lumsden, to members of his family back in England. His observations show just how whiskey and the plight of the Irish were so inextricably intertwined. He wrote on April 15, 1816:

"In a detachment with another officer and 32 men 20 miles from Derry...except Potatoes and Eggs we cannot get an article of subsistence nearer than headquarters. Out every night searching for private Stills and generally not in vain...illicit distillation appears their only means of subsistence and yet the fines arising from it have actually ruined them.

"They are now desperate...If another law of felony is imposed (illicit distillation) will be found insufficient to stop...for transportation cannot deter men who are conscious their situation may be better but cannot be worse. The voice of kindness is so great a stranger to their ear that the first word of it awakens their utmost gratitude."

And on August 6, 1816:

"I entered (this country) with a disposition to esteem the inhabitants but this atrocious Murder (of Norton Butler of Grouse Hall, Carndonagh) has jaundiced my mind against the Bastardy of Scotch craft and Irish ferocity...His murder was marked with particular ferocity...after the two balls had er~~red him...the fellow rushed forward and put his bayonet through his thigh entering four

inches into the ground. In the struggle the bayonet broke and left him pinioned to the ground...His death was occasioned by his exertion to put down illicit distillation...the murderer is known and protected by the inhabitants and though the rewards for his detection are large, yet nothing will induce the infamous Crew to give him up. I was all last night searching for him.

"A few days since I went out on Revenue duty with a Mr Cailaghan, Surveyor of Excise. He and a gauger galloped after a man who was running off with a still. They left my view...(twenty minutes

Left
*Poteen-makers
tend their still in
Co. Donegal at
the turn of the
century.*

later) I found Mr Callaghan to all appearances
dead, his skull fractured with stones and entirely
unable to speak or move.

"This country is ruined, it is the station of
Poverty – all who can are flying from the
approaching ruin and hope in America to find
hope and plenty."

Norton Butler had been one of the most active
law agents in the battle against illicit distilling and
before Lumsden's gruesome discovery, previous
attempts had been made upon his life. The area
Lumsden and Butler had been trying to police was

located in Inishowen, the most northern tip of Donegal, close to Malin Head and a region which enjoyed a reputation with regard to Irish whiskey as Glenlivet did in the Scottish Highlands. A few years earlier in Inishowen, Aeneas Coffey, who later went on to become both Inspector General of Excise and the inventor of a continuous still which bears his name to this day, narrowly escaped with his life after a north Donegal illicit distilling militia set about him with such venom he was fortunate to live and achieve later fame. He recalled that "they fractured my skull, left my body one mass of contusion, and gave me two bayonet wounds, one of which completely perforated my thigh. I owed my life to the rapid approach of the military party from which I had imprudently wandered a few hundred yards..."

Thankfully it has been many years since such horrors awaited those whose job it was to put down illicit distilling and today are totally unheard of. Where the British soldier and government agent failed, two major events helped reduce this traffic in Ireland. One was the extraordinary zeal of the temperance campaigner Father Mathew and the other was the gradual decline of the peasant status with more people being allowed to own their own land. Able now to produce cash crops rather than whiskey, many former illicit distillers decided on a more legal way of life as Victorian Christian values and expectancy hardened.

At the time of Lumsden the poteen distilled was whiskey, or would have been had it been allowed to mature. Then it was drunk as many days or weeks old as it is now years. One of the biggest problems, though, was the making of the malt. It was common for the illicit distiller to leave a sack of grain in a stream, hoping it would not be detected, and allow it to dry in various places about his home, even under his bed if it had legs. Because of peat being used almost exclusively in the quick drying of the malt, any whiskey produced in Ireland with a peaty aroma and taste was called "poteen flavoured".

Because of the time and trouble involved in the malting process potatoes became more commonly used by illicit distillers and in the 1880s molasses

---

BUNRATTY EXPORT POTCHEEN   40 PER CENT ABV

NOSE: In some ways nearer to poteen than new spirit from large stills, there is an odd, sugary sweetness which clings about the grain. It does lack the behind-the-counter poteen fruitiness and harshness, but is still very pleasant.

TASTE: Very sweet, grainy and quite full-tasting with a slight oiliness. By comparison, poteen I tasted in the hills attacks the tongue and roof of the mouth without mercy and leaves a more complex, though usually less-smooth residual feel.

FINISH: Thinnish for poteen but with a pleasant spiciness which peps it all up. The malt effect is rather single-layered.

COMMENTS: A sanitised but still moderately enjoyable version of the stuff you find from nameless friends of friends. It would be better at full strength, though, as this is rather too soft. Available from duty free in Ireland and now even from Fortnum & Mason in London's Piccadilly.

was found more than useful on account of the fact that it helped produce fermentable solids.

The stuff made by the poteen-maker I visited in the mountains of Donegal, the perpetual heartland of illicit distilling, was based on just that. Today there is perhaps more hooch made in Galway than any other part of Ireland but it is all similar to my man's. He used an old copper still. Now, like others, he uses a Burco boiler: "cheap to run, twice as efficient". Although the boiler is stainless steel, vitally, the condensing coil is still made of copper. But even here the distiller is keeping tradition alive in a way: last century Irish tinkers used to sell stills made from tin.

His recipe consists of two stones of unmalted barley, four stones of brown sugar, a gallon of treacle, a gallon of syrup, a box of apples to help fermentation and add flavour, and lastly, a pound of yeast.

Where once the game of the distiller could be given away by the small plume of smoke which would rise from his bothy like a beacon into the sky, these days he has to be careful of his suppliers. Many an illicit distiller has been turned in by a shopkeeper in return for a small reward. This Donegal distiller gets his materials from trusted friends. In return they receive a bottle or two of the stuff.

What he makes is a lot better than the poteen I have tasted from other illicit distillers in Ireland. He has triple distilled it, so although fiery, it remains light and soft with a fruitiness which possibly derives from the apples. Another curious link with the past here: it has been thought possible that a cider brandy may have been made in Ireland in the Middle Ages when a number of cider makers from Gloucestershire emigrated across the Irish sea.

The still is in a tiny ante-room in the kitchen and his entire output for a year is little more than 20 bottles. You will not find any of this whiskey on the duty free shelves of Cork and Dublin airports like one "poteen" that is from Bunratty Mead & Co, whose owner, Oliver Dillon, claims to produce in County Clare the world's only commercial poteen. Although the company cannot sell it in the Republic, the fact the Irish Government takes money off the distiller in taxation from his profits, somehow runs contrary to the spirit of the spirit!

Commercial enterprises apart, there is currently a renaissance of totally illegal poteen-making in Ireland with, for example, illicit stills working out of Cork and Dublin, cities where they had long been extinct. But no one has any real idea just how many poteen-makers are on the loose. The distiller up on his small holding in Donegal told me he knows four others, and those four probably know four others and so on.

"Don't you see," he points out, "It's not just a case of keeping the tradition alive. It's more the keeping of the tradition of sticking two fingers up to the authorities for not letting us do what all Irishmen consider a God-given right."

CHAPTER SIX

WHERE TO VISIT

A T FIRST GLANCE, IT LOOKS AS IF THERE IS NOT MUCH OF A CHOICE. IN THE WHOLE OF IRELAND THERE ARE ONLY THREE DISTILLERIES, ONE OF WHICH, COOLEY, IS NOT ALWAYS IN PRODUCTION.

Opposite
The basalt columns of the Giant's Causeway on the north Antrim coast are just a few miles from the Bushmills Distillery.

Another, Midleton, is out of bounds to the general tourist which leaves Bushmills as the single working distillery to welcome people with open arms. Pretty puny when you compare that with all that Scotland has to offer. There, you can choose from dozens of distilleries with visitor facilities ranging from Bowmore on Islay to Highland Park in Orkney with Glenfiddich on Speyside.

But in fact, Ireland is a little green gem for the whiskey enthusiast. It may have only the one working distillery to inspect but it boasts two ancient distilleries – one at Midleton, the other at Kilbeggan – which date from the late 18th and early 19th centuries and are each preserved in aspic. They have a charm and sense of history that leaves them peerless throughout the world.

All three distilleries could not be further apart. Bushmills is found on the north Antrim coast, just two miles from the eighth natural wonder of the world, the Giant's Causeway, part of a series of peculiar geological features formed by the cooling of volcanic basalt rock. The Antrim coast is one of the most glorious and least known treasures of the British Isles and its softly sculpted hills and mountains, which lie just inland, are well worth a visit before or after your tour of the distillery. The Bushmills Distillery stands proud and classical, its twin fishscale-tiled pagodas marking where the malting once took place, as much a focal point to the old works as floodlight pylons are to a soccer stadium. The whiskey distillery annually welcomes over 70,000 people and has become one of Northern Ireland's biggest attractions. This year the building of its new visitor's centre was completed, with a former warehouse being converted into a reception area before guided tours begin. These invariably finish with a glass of 10-year-old malt or the masterful Black Bush in a bar beside the museum which holds relics from not only Bushmills, but the lost distillery of Coleraine.

To then reach the other working distillery at Midleton from Bushmills you have to travel the entire length of the country. The journey can be made down through the centre of Ireland, or down the west coast, but the roads are not good. Alternatively you could go along the east coast via Dublin where there are the remains of the old Power's Distillery, and on the other side of the Liffey, taking up part of what remains of a warehouse attached to the old Jameson Bow Street Distillery, is The Irish Whiskey Corner. Owned, developed and recently completed by Irish Distillers, it is next door to their current head office and is the only place in Eire's capital which has been given over to the country's long and proud distilling tradition.

Outside The Whiskey Corner is a still from the Power's Distillery, and another inside which once hissed and steamed within the Bow Street complex. The centre is part museum and part exhibition with a dummy cooper and cut-out maltmen giving some idea of how whiskey is made. There are also mounted photographs showing the history of Jameson's Bow Street Distillery and an audio visual centre to take people through the whiskey-making process. And, of course, there is the Ball O'Malt bar, where, after one of the conducted tours, you will be allowed to sample a range of whiskeys from around the world in order to educate your palate to the joys of drinking Irish. It is certainly an enjoyable place to spend an hour and learn something about Ireland's distilling heritage.

And while at Bow Street, and if you are not squeamish, it is worth enquiring to see if you can gain access to the famous crypt of St Michan's Church, where the strange subterranean microclimate has ensured that the corpses have remained in a mummified state for many centuries. This is where Alfred Barnard began his journey of Ireland's distilleries in 1885; it was a place of great renown, even over a century ago.

On leaving Dublin it is then worth taking the N4 into the Irish midlands, picking up the N6 to Kilbeggan. The countryside is flat and lush; the sight of Kilbeggan Distillery as it first comes into view, however, is one which will be indelibly stamped on your mind's eye.

I have already devoted a section of this book to the history of Locke's distillery at Kilbeggan. With the sun reflecting off the River Brosna, and the water-wheel dark against the distillery's 18th-century whitewashed wall, it is truly one of the most gladdening visions of Ireland. Inside are the same implements which were in use from the last century up until its demise in the 1950s. A trust has been set up to keep the buildings not only in this same breathtaking condition, but also to carry out whatever restoration work is possible. There are hopes the water-wheel will again be driving some of the machinery and plant which still lie dusty, redundant but resplendent within the ancient distillery.

From Kilbeggan it is just a six-mile drive to Tullamore where the remains of the old distillery can still be seen. South-east from Kilbeggan and away from the direction of Cork is another gem, Monasterevan Distillery. Barnard accompanied his description of the distillery with a drawing. The main body of the offices are so well-preserved today, that I found I was able to drive up and park beside it without any confirmation from the locals that I had the right place.

The inside of the distillery, containing some of the most extraordinary and beautiful industrial architecture in Ireland is on private land behind a shop and not open to public access. But although the distillery has been silent since 1921, you can still make out much from Barnard's drawing, including Brennan's Bar which, typically for Ireland, doubles up as a store which you have to walk through before you get to the serious bit. But it is another Monasterevan bar, Mooney's, on Main Street, effectively the Tullamore road, which is most sought after by the whiskey lover. In a well-locked cabinet inside the snug is a bottle of Monasterevan from the last century, unopened and full of golden promise. It is the last remaining bottle of Monasterevan known to exist.

Elsewhere in Ireland it is possible to find remains of desolate, dilapidated distilleries. But there is one, above all, which is a mecca for the Irish whiskey drinker. Midleton.

The history of the old distillery is given elsewhere but nearly all that Barnard saw for himself is still there, including, in pristine condition, the earliest distillery fire engine known. Just as at The Whiskey Corner, there is also a large pot still from the old Jameson Bow Street Distillery outside the entrance.

Money is being spent on making it easier for people to walk around the site; in so doing I just hope they don't fill in a rut which is found below a very low level bridge. That rut was formed over a period of 70 years by distillery workmen riding their bikes under the bridge, to and from work, and ducking to their handlebars. If they got the line wrong a nasty crack in the head and concussion was a guaranteed certainty.

Elsewhere around the old distillery grounds multilingual audiovisual booths have been set up to tell people in which part of Midleton they have found themselves. The tourist attractions are far more high-tech than the distillery ever was.

Back inside the distillery is the only bar I know which stocks every brand of whiskey made by the company, including the sherry-rich Distillery Reserve, a heavyweight 12-year-old. It cannot be bought anywhere else.

It will be interesting to see if Irish Distillers make the new Midleton Distillery equally as accessible to the public as is the old one. There are no plans as yet, but watch this space.

Sometimes I am asked by whiskey enthusiasts who have only a short time in Ireland where to go for a one-off visit. I am often tempted to recommend a trip to Bushmills, since you can see the men at work and enjoy the north Antrim distillery as part of a larger and quite beautiful whole.

Or a visit to Midleton, which is so antiquated, and where it takes some believing that it was worked in this manner until as recently as 1975. If it's Dublin, it has to be The Irish Whiskey Corner, because as well as the displays and the whiskey tasting, you can also see what remains of Bow Street Distillery. This is an absolute must.

But for something that is just too special to miss, it has to be Kilbeggan. Owned by a trust, it is one of Irish whiskey's "neutrals". True, part of the site is owned by Cooley Distillery, who have used the warehousing to mature their own make, and the stills of Tullamore, which can be seen from inside the distillery, belong to Cooley as well. When you gaze on this wonderful piece of whiskey history, you cannot help but feel that it belongs not just to Ireland, but to every man and woman from every whiskey distillery who, over the course of the last two centuries, spent their lives making Irish pot still whiskey, one of, and for many, the most glorious spirit in the world.

Old Bushmills Distillery
Co. Antrim, Northern Ireland

| Apr–Oct | Mon–Sat, 0930–1730 |
| | Sun, 1200–1730 |

Regular tours each day, last tour 1600

| Nov–Mar | Mon–Fri |

Regular tours, ring for details of times
telephone   (012657) 31521

The Irish Whiskey Corner
Bow Street, Dublin, Eire

| May–Oct | Mon–Sun |

Ring for details of tour times.

| Nov–Apr | Mon–Fri |

One tour a day at 1530
telephone   (01) 872 5566

The Jameson Heritage Centre
Midleton, Co. Cork, Eire

| mid-Mar–Oct | Mon–Sun, 1000–1600 |

Regular tours, ring for details of times
telephone   (021) 613594

GLOSSARY

Aqua vitae   Latin term for "water of life". Usually distilled from wine. Whiskey was also called this by clerics for the purposes of official documentation.

Blending   Process/art form of mixing malt or pot still whiskey with grain whiskey.

Brewing   Act by infusion and, with the aid of yeast, of producing alcoholic liquids from sugars present in a solution containing fermented grains.

Cask   Barrel which contains maturing spirit or whiskey.

Coffey Still   Patent still invented by Aeneas Coffey allowing the continuous distillation of wash.

Column Still   Apparatus designed for the continues production of alcoholic spirit..

Draff   Spent solids of grain, or dregs, from the brewing process which are removed from the mash tun and usually sold on as rich feed for farm livestock.

Feints   Impure spirit produced from the tail end of the second distillation, and which needs to be re-distilled to make suitable for filling.

Fermentation   Explosive period during the brewing process when sugar-rich liquid wort reacts with yeast.

Fermenters   An Irish term for wash backs.

Fillings   Term applied to new spirit filled into cask before being warehoused for maturation.

Foreshots   Oily spirit produced at the start of each "run" from the stills.

Gauger The old name given to an exciseman, whose job it was to put down illicit distillation and smuggling.

Grain Whiskey Whiskey produced from column stills, usually from wheat or maize but with a small amount of malted barley to aid fermentation.

Grist Crushed grains, in the case of Irish pot still, a mixture of unmalted and malted barley which, is added to hot water called liquor in the first step of the brewing process.

Malt Barley which has been artificially germinated by first steeping in cold water then spread thinly to dry and allowing shoots to develop.

Marrying Period in which whiskeys from more than one distillery or set of stills react with each other to form a blend or vatting before bottling.

Mashing Process by which the grist is added to hot water to dissolve all the fermentable sugar-like carbohydrates.

Mash Tun Large metal container in which the grist is added to the liquor (hot water) for mashing to be carried out. The liquid formed is called wort.

Maturation When a spirit is filled into a cask it reacts over a period of years with chemicals within the wood, to form its ever-changing character. The longer the whiskey is kept in the wood the greater the wood influence will be. Whiskey only matures in wood, never in glass. So the age of a whiskey on the bottle shows the age of the youngest whiskey used in the bottling. It does not get any older once bottled.

Mouth Feel	Term applied to a whiskey on the effect it has on the palate. It could be smooth, fiery, soft, light, cloying and so on.
Peat	Organic material formed by decaying matter found in boggy land and when cut and dried perfect as a burning fuel. Traditionally used in the making of whiskey for the drying of malt.
Poteen (or *poiteen*)	An illicit spirit made once from malted barley sometimes from potato, but today more likely from molasses.
Pot Stills	Bulbous copper containers in which the wash, produced from either pure malted barley or a mixture of malted and unmalted barley, is heated until vapours containing alcohol rises and separates from the water.
Pot Still Whiskey	Traditional name given to Irish whiskey which is made from a mixture of malted and unmalted barley. Once, it also contained small quantities of oats and rye. Not to be confused with single malt, or pure malt.
Run	Colourless, alcohol-rich liquid, which flows from the still after having passed through the worm.
Shebeen	Illegal drinking house, usually located in the most desolate areas of Ireland, but also occasionally in towns. Here poteen is consumed and sometimes sold by the bottle.
Single Malt	Malt whiskey from just one distillery and not mixed with either grain or pot still whiskey.

Uisce Beatha Celtic name for "water of life", and the derivative term for whiskey: *uisce* was corrupted to *uisgey* and thus whiskey or whisky.

Vatting Mixing together of identical style whiskey from the same distillery but from different casks. Not to be confused with a vatted whiskey – a mixture of malt whisky from more than one distillery.

Wash Beer-like liquid which has undergone the fermentation process and is ready to be pumped into the wash still for the first distillation.

Wash backs Sometimes called fermenters in Ireland, they can be made from either wood, or stainless steel. They are massive vessels which hold the fermenting liquid as it changes from wort to wash.

Wood All whiskey in the major whiskey-producing nations has to be matured, by law, in oak. See casks and maturation.

Worm Coiled copper tube in which the vaporised alcohols from the stills condense to form the spirit which matures into whiskey.

Wort Liquid high in dissolved sugars and containing the malt. Goes through a cooling process before being pumped into the wash backs for the next stage in brewing: fermentation.

Yeast Tiny plant organisms which feed off sugar and form alcohol and carbon dioxide as by-products. Added to the wort in the mash tuns to aid fermentation.

INDEX

ACKNOWLEDGMENTS

It goes without saying that a book like this cannot be written without the aid of a great many people. On top of the great fun I have had visiting Ireland in the past, the extra kindness I received while researching this book will always be cherished. In particular I would like to thank: Ms Ide Ni Thuama of the Royal Irish Academy; Dr Richard Sharp, Reader in Diplomatic Studies, Oxford University; John Burgass, Librarian, Merton College, Oxford; Miss P Kernaghan, Deputy Keeper of the Records, Public Record Office of Northern Ireland and Ms E D L Lumsden for their kind permission in allowing me to quote from the Samual Lumsden papers D649/11-14; Jack Gamble of Emerald Isle Books, Belfast; John Ryan, Barry Walsh, Michael Borre and Cathal O'Farrell of Irish Distillers, Dublin; Barry Crockett at Midleton Distillery; Douglas Deane, the North Mall bottling plant, Cork; Frank McHardy, Denis Higgins, John McLernon and the gatekeeper at Bushmills Distillery; Caroline Davey (formerly) and Heidi Cohu, now of Campbell Distillers; John Harte and Noel Sweeney of Cooley Distillers; Robert Mitchell and Peter Dunne of Mitchell & Son, Dublin; Kevin Abrook of Cantrell & Cochrane, Dublin and Joe Scally of Irish Mist at Tullamore; Gordon Wright and Neil Clapperton, of Wm Cadenhead, Campbeltown and Edinburgh; Dr Nicholas Morgan of the United Distillers Archive, Edinburgh; Jonathan Driver of United Distillers, London; Jamie Graham and the Board of Directors of Berry Bros. & Rudd, London; Peter O'Connor of Baileys, Dublin; Tom Keaveney of Gilbey's, Ireland; Paul Hyland of Mooney's and P J Brennan of Brennan's, Monasterevan; Eddie Nevin of The Vineyard, Galway; Philip and Mark Russell of The Elk, Dundonald; my man John, the illicit distiller somewhere in Co. Donegal; Morton McKnight and Maynard Hanna of Distillery FC; Bea Tom of The Buena Vista Cafe, San Francisco; Oliver Dillon of the Bunratty Mead Co. and Michael Sohel of Pondicherry International, Leeds; Mr Brian Lawson, former sexton of St Michan's Church, Dublin; Margaret Bridgman of Halewood Vintners, West Yorks; John Layden and the sixth form Latin students of Wellingborough School; Billy Walker of Burn Stewart Distillers, Airdrie; Dr Jim Swann of R R Tatlock and Thomson, Glasgow, and Jimmy Lang, Becky Calcraft, Howard Buchanan, Sue Westhall and Diana Crook. My very warmest thanks go to Christina Holmes, whose late husband John did so much to record the history of Monasterevan Distillery, for being such a charming and good-natured guide around the remains of the old distillery at a time of great personal sadness. Thanks also to Michael Nagl for providing a selection of old advertisements and labels from his collection of Irish drink memorabilia.

Most of all I would like to give a big hug and kiss to my young son James for being such a funny and understanding companion on our sojourn around Ireland's past and present distilleries, and for all the time he has merrily got on with things at home allowing me to somehow complete this book in time for publication. I'm also indebted to my other wonderful children, Tabitha and David, for likewise so uncomplainingly taking second place to this labour of love when there was vitally important shopping and cricket practice to be done.